AMERICAN LITERATURE

IN PARODY

American
Literature
In Parody

A Collection of Parody, Satire, and Literary Burlesque

of American Writers Past and Present

EDITED BY R O B E R T P. F A L K

Illustrated by

BURGES GREEN

TWAYNE PUBLISHERS

New York

To
JANE, HAROLD,
AND EUGENIA FALK

Acknowledgments

It is not easy to remember all those who, during the several years of collecting and planning the present volume, have helped me with encouragement and advice of many kinds. Among those I can recall who have taken an interest in the book or have given me specific leads and suggestions, it is a pleasure to express my appreciation to the following colleagues and associates of mine at the University of California: John J. Espey, Majl Ewing, Glenn Gosling, Wayland Hand, Leon Howard, Blake R. Nevius, Ada B. Nisbet, Donald Pizer, John R. Ross, and Wilbur J. Smith. Also my thanks to the following for good counsel and moral support: Paul Bechtner, Walter Blair, John A. Clark, Peter De Vries, Clifton Fadiman, Holman Hamilton, Gilbert Highet, Hallett D. Smith, Frank Sullivan, and James Thurber.

For permission to reprint the copyrighted selections in this volume, I wish to thank the following individuals and publishers:

"Poem for Benjamin Franklin's Birthday" from WHAT THE QUEEN SAID by Stoddard King. Copyright 1926 by Doubleday and Company, Inc.

"The Late Benjamin Franklin" from SKETCHES NEW AND OLD by Mark Twain. By permission of Harper and Brothers.

"The Shrike and the Chipmunks" by James Thurber. Copyright 1939 James Thurber. Originally published in *The New Yorker.*

"Wise Saws and Modern Instances" from CYNIC'S WORD BOOK by Ambrose Bierce. By permission of Albert and Charles Boni, Inc.

"Cooper's Defects," "Stilted Dialogue," "The Broken Twig Series," "The Delicate Art of the Forest" from IN DEFENSE OF HARRIET SHELLEY by Mark Twain. Copyright 1897 by Harper and Brothers.

"Muck-a-Muck, a Modern Indian Novel after Cooper" by Bret Harte. By permission of Houghton Mifflin Company.

"A Garland of Ibids for Van Wyck Brooks" by Frank Sullivan. By permission of the author and *The New Yorker.*

"A Literary Bombshell" by Mark Twain. From MARK TWAIN A BIOGRAPHY. Copyright 1912 by Harper and Brothers. Copyright 1940 by Dora L. Paine.

"Mrs. Judge Jenkins" by Bret Harte. By permission of Houghton Mifflin Company.

"The Retort Transcendental" from THE SECOND TREE FROM THE CORNER by E. B. White. Copyright 1953 by E. B. White. Published by Harper and Brothers.

"The Vulgarity of Poe" from MUSIC AT NIGHT by Aldous Huxley. Copyright 1930, 1931 by Aldous Huxley. Published by Harper and Brothers.

"The Willows" by Bret Harte. By permission of Houghton Mifflin Company.

"A Poe-'em of Passion" from A BRONCO PEGASUS by C. F. Lummis. By permission of Mrs. Turbese L. Fiske. Published by Houghton Mifflin Company.

"Ulabel Lume" by Barbara Angell. By permission of the author.

"A Classic Waits for Me" from THE SECOND TREE FROM THE CORNER by E. B. White. Copyright 1944 by E. B. White. Published by Harper and Brothers.

"In Darkest James" from IMAGINARY OBLIGATIONS by Frank Moore Colby. Copyright 1904 by Dodd, Mead and Company. Copyright renewed 1932 by Harriet Colby.

"A Magnificent but Painful Hippopotamus" from BOON by H. G. Wells. By permission of Mrs. Marjorie Wells.

"A Limerick by Henry James" from A PARODY ANTHOLOGY by Carolyn Wells. Copyright 1904 by Charles Scribner's Sons, 1932 by Carolyn Houghton Wells. By permission of the publishers.

"How Love Came to General Grant" from A PARODY OUTLINE OF HISTORY by Donald Ogden Stewart. Copyright 1921 by Doubleday and Company, Inc.

"The Norris Plan" from IN THE WORST POSSIBLE TASTE by Corey Ford. Copyright 1932 by Corey Ford. By permission of the publishers, Charles Scribner's Sons.

"Hot Stuff in the Nineties" from WHAT THE QUEEN SAID by Stoddard King. Copyright 1926 by Doubleday and Company, Inc.

"The Treasurer's Report" from BENCHLEY BESIDE HIMSELF by Robert Benchley. Copyright 1930 by Robert C. Benchley. Published by Harper and Brothers.

"Salesman of Salvation" from BABBITT by Sinclair Lewis. Copyright 1922 by Harcourt, Brace and Company, Inc. Copyright renewed 1950 by Sinclair Lewis.

"If Gray Had Had to Write His Elegy in the Cemetery of Spoon River Instead of in That of Stoke Poges" and "The Parodist's Impression of the Impressionists" from COLLECTED PARODIES and TRICKS OF THE TRADE by J. C. Squire. By permission of the author.

"The Grackle and the Pear Tree" from TREE WITH A BIRD IN IT by Margaret Widdemer. By permission of the author. Published by Harcourt, Brace and Company, Inc.

"Carl Sandburg Hates the Stuff," "The Moist Land" from YEAR IN YOU'RE OUT by Samuel Hoffenstein. By permission of Liveright Publishing Corp. Copyright 1930 by Samuel Hoffenstein.

"Homage to Ezra Pound" by Gilbert Highet. By permission of the author.

"Einstein Among the Coffee Cups," "Edgar Guest Considers the Old Woman in the Shoe" from COLLECTED PARODIES by Louis Untermeyer. Copyright 1926 by Harcourt, Brace and Company, Inc. Copyright renewed 1954 by Louis Untermeyer.

"The Love Song of F. Scott Fitzgerald" by John A. Clark. By permission of the author.

"Life Is a Bowl of Eugene O'Neills" by Frank Sullivan. By permission of the author.

"Shad Ampersand, A Novel of Time and the Writer," "The Education of Henry Apley" by Wolcott Gibbs. Published by Random House, Inc.

"For Whom the Gong Sounds" from SOAP BEHIND THE EARS by Cornelia Otis Skinner. Copyright 1941 by Cornelia Otis Skinner. By permission of Dodd, Mead and Company.

"Of Nothing and the Wolfe" by Clifton Fadiman. By permission of the author. Reprinted from *The American Spectator*.

"Requiem for a Noun, or Intruder in the Dusk" by Peter De Vries. By permission of the author.

Contents

* *Title supplied by the editor.*

* *Title supplied by the editor.*

* *Title supplied by the editor.*

AMERICAN LITERATURE

IN PARODY

Some highly-regarded savants of an earlier and more principled generation than our own gave currency to the opinion that the writer of parody was a rather shabby fellow practising an irreverent and parasitic art and an enemy within the gates of the true, the beautiful, and the good. According to this standard, the collector of parody, having not even the excuse of expressing his own aesthetic ego, must be one of the most abandoned of literary riff-raff. It may be unnecessary in our enlightened era to say anything in self-defense for indulging in so irresponsible a pastime as editing parodies, but if it were, I would have little to say. It would be futile to deny that the parodist is out for a laugh at somebody's expense or that successful parody can have a damaging effect upon the uninitiated. For the present volume I seek only the audience of the experienced who need no advice or justification from me. As for the uninitiated, they will endure, having little interest in so shady a profession as parody anyway. For me, however, the "problem" of parody is resolved as easily as Dr. Johnson disposed of the problem of free will—all theory is against it and all experience is for it.

Parody is both a form of literary humor and a branch of criticism. As humor, it is probably wiser not to explain it or attempt to rationalize it. As criticism, however, one may venture a few generalizations. For one thing, it addresses itself not to original qualities of a work of art, but ridicules the pretentious or eccentric and helps separate the wheat from the chaff. In the case of Poe, for instance, a good parody will point up that "two-fifths" of his work of which Lowell spoke:

> Here comes Poe with his raven like Barnaby Rudge
> Three-fifths of him genius and two-fifths sheer fudge.

True genius has so magnetic an appeal that it will almost instantaneously ripen into cliché and give birth to a swarm of imitators. The parodist may aim his shafts at these copies rather than at the original. Or he may address himself to elements of conventionalism within an already acknowledged classic. More often than not a parody will expose with wit and deftness what is generally agreed to be second-rate. Thus the writer of parody is not without his useful function—to seize upon sham and pretense in the literary world and point out the difference between originality and flim-flam. In the larger view parody may even presage a change in literary taste or form by placing in comic perspective a mannerism of thought or technique which has begun to decay. By the negative means of humorous criticism, parody may help to single out the enduring qualities of a work of art.

Ezra Pound, in his *ABC of Reading,* has some advice for teachers endeavoring to introduce their pupils to the art of reading verse:

Let him parody some poem he finds ridiculous, either because of falsity in the statement, or falsity in the disposition of the writer, or for pretentiousness of one kind or another, or for any other reason that strikes his risible faculties, his sense of irony.

Such an exercise, says Pound, might test both the poem parodied and the parodist. The joke might be on either one. Furthermore, this exercise should help to distinguish good parodies from bad, for the students should be asked to recognize

Whether the parody exposes a real defect, or merely makes use of an author's mechanism to expose a more trivial content.

Albert Jay Nock likewise stressed the values of parody as literary criticism when he ranked Bret Harte as one of the world's best practitioners of the art. He said,

If I were trying to interest a modern student in these distinguished Victorians (Dickens, Bronte and others) I am not sure but that I would approach the task by way of Harte's parodies.

Wolcott Gibbs, who has written some of the best modern parodies, writes in the introduction to *Season in the Sun* that a good parody should contain a certain amount of real criticism of what the author is saying as well as his manner of saying it. The best parody, however, differs from other kinds of literary criticism in that it breathes the very spirit of the style or idea it seeks to criticize. It approaches its subject from the inside, not from without, and will have nothing to do with academic yardsticks or arbitrary measures of literary excellence. In pointing the finger at weakness, the parodist does so in the very idiom of the original. To quote Mr. Gibbs once more, parody should be "pitched so little above (or below) the key of the original that an intelligent critic, on being read passages from both, might be honestly confused." This is a way of saying that subtlety is one of the fundamental qualities of superior parody. If it is true that imitation is the sincerest form of flattery, then surely parody at its best is the subtlest kind of imitation. It must ring true not only to external tricks of style in the original, but also to the essential figure in the carpet, as Max Beerbohm's classic parody of James so skillfully does. At the same time everything must be converted to the humorous end. Successful parody holds in equilibrium two opposing attitudes towards its subject—satire and sympathy. It involves an amalgamation of the satiric mood with a thoroughgoing understanding of the style it burlesques. At its best it holds the razor edge between admiration and ridicule. To accomplish this requires superior art and mimetic talent.

Is parody, as someone has suggested, now out of fashion? Has its vogue declined since the passing of the literary debunkers of the 1920's when a certain bullish confidence in the basic health of American purposes underlay the noisy disparagements of Mencken & Co.? It may be that the challenge from abroad to the democratic way of life has put us upon the defensive and rendered the satirist of American literary gods an object of suspicion, if not investigation. If so, it is time we reasserted the American prerogative to laugh at ourselves. Like other forms of humor good parody will always have an audience. When it is directed toward our own literary traditions, it can be one of the healthy signs of the readiness of a democracy to criticize its own forms and methods of expression. The present century has been particularly fruitful in parody writing, more so than any similar period of our history. Such humorists as Corey Ford, James Thurber, Frank Sullivan, Wolcott Gibbs, and Donald Ogden Stewart have raised the level of the art in this country to that of the great English parodists of the past century. If the conditions of the past decade have not been conducive to the light-hearted mood necessary for the production of good parody, one may confidently urge that the situation is temporary and that parody will reassert its claims to attention and interest among people who read.

Collections of parody and literary imitation have appeared from time to time. Some have aimed at completeness, like the six-volume colossus of Walter B. Hamilton, published in the 1880's, where the reader is deluged with hundreds of parodies of English and American classics. Others, smaller and more discriminating, have sought to select only the superior examples of the art. The nonsense anthologies of Carolyn Wells, the parody collection of J. C. Squire, treasuries of humorous prose and verse, the individual parody-books of Louis Untermeyer, Corey Ford, Donald Ogden Stewart—all have found delighted readers and wide approval. These volumes generally fall into two types—original parody collections by a single author like Corey Ford's *John Riddell Murder Case, A Philo Vance Parody,* or Donald Ogden Stewart's *A Parody Outline of History* where the selections are grouped around a central theme or narrative thread, and the more conventional anthologies of parody like those edited by Carolyn Wells or J. C. Squire in which the selections are drawn from the wide literature of parody in the interests of preserving the best.

The present collection, however, has a somewhat different purpose quite apart from the pleasure and humor in the selections themselves. By arranging the parodies around a central theme, the history of American letters, it has been my intention to test the values of parody as criticism and to provide a kind of parody-handbook to American literature. Thus, I have gathered together those parodies and satirical treatments of the American classics which, when taken together, produce an over-all burlesque commentary upon our literary past and present. Most of our recognizable writing techniques and attitudes have at one time or other passed through the hands of the parodist. Many of the finest, as well as the best-selling, of American poets and prose writers have found themselves for good or ill in caricature. A large proportion of these parodies are pedestrian exercises, written to exploit some passing fashion, and are hardly worth reprinting. But there are among them many skillful instances of the *genre.* When adequately selected and arranged they provide a minority critical report, as it were, on American literary methods and a body of criticism which, taken in the large, is well worth preserving. I have arranged them chronologically by authors or schools of writing including parodies from any English sources when I thought they were funny and when they helped place the American literary tradition in the perspective of the caricaturist. Some are well known and have seen more than one reprinting; others have not, to my knowledge, been republished from original sources or received the currency they deserve.

Of all the American classic writers probably Longfellow and Poe have been the target of the greatest number of parodies with Whitman a close third. A selection from the canon of parodies on these three poets must be made with considerable care. Most of them are best left to the oblivion of the unread. Only a few bright passages have survived from a vast desert of verses ringing the changes on "Hiawatha," "The Village Blacksmith," "A Psalm of Life," "The Raven," "Annabel Lee," and "Leaves of Grass." "A London Legend" by Harry Wandsworth Shortfellow was published in 1856 subtitled (a bit lamely) "The Song of Drop o' Wather." This parody of 120 lines (no verse parody should be that long!) chronicled the seamy life of a London slum child from his birth of a drunken mother through a lurid career of crime, to his final departure to Australia. But the sing-song meter of "Hiawatha" was perhaps too easy a mark to challenge the first-rate parodist. Lewis Carroll apologized for attempting it in his "Hiawatha's Photographing" in which the epic rhythms are used to laugh at the then newly-invented art of photography. Phoebe Cary aped the high sentence of "A Psalm of Life" more successfully, as she likewise punctured the airy sentiment of "The Day Is Done." C. S. Calverly, who wrote many fine parodies of British poets, contributed a good one on "Voices in the Night," and Wyndham Lewis' prose burlesque of "The Case of the Village Blacksmith" stands out from an otherwise drab procession of imitations of the patriarch of American verse.

As in the case of Longfellow, the collector of Poe parodies needs to use the pruning shears liberally. Imitations of "The Raven" are legion as anyone who has glanced through Hamilton's collection is aware. A few of them, however, are superior and of these I would place at the top of the list C. L. Edson's travesty of the excessive riming device in "The Raven." The unconscious burlesques of the Poe style in Thomas Holly Chivers' "Isadore" and other poems are highly amusing though for a somewhat different reason intended, as they were, as serious poems. Huxley's well-known essay on Poe's "vulgarity" contains a brief parody illustration of

17

the main argument. "Annabel Lee" brought forth, among many take-offs, the excellent "A Poe-'em of Passion" by C. F. Lummis and Tom Hood's "The Cannibal Flea," but "The Bells" only produced innumerable dullish variations of such possible puns as "the pills," "The girls," "the bills," and so forth. The best and only good prose parody of Poe is that of Grace Greenwood whose "A Tale of Horror by E.A.P." ably burlesqued the grotesque tale.

Whitman parodies have been collected by Henry Saunders and many of them are familiar to followers of the bard. Of them I have chosen Richard Grant White's and H. C. Bunner's as among the most successful. The long unselective catalogues, the breathless puffs of exhilaration, the chest-thumping, the French words where the English would do as well—these traits appear in most of the Whitman parodies in more or less skillful combination. As Bunner put it in his caricature of the Whitmanian pose:

This is my exhibition—it is the greatest show on earth—there is no charge for admission. All you have to pay me is to take in my romanza.

Good Parodies of Emerson and the transcendental style are by no means easy to find. His most frequently imitated poem, "Brahma," provoked a few fairly good burlesque versions of the mistiness of the Emersonian style and Bayard Taylor attempted a parody of him in his "Diversions of the Echo Club." But for the most part the light approach to transcendentalism lay in sharply-worded essays by Poe and Lowell or in later satirical portraiture of Bluestocking reformers and feminist inspirational lecturers such as Henry James' sketch of Miss Birdseye from the *Bostonians* or Sinclair Lewis's Mrs. Mudge of the Higher Illumination League from *Babbitt*. Thoreau, strangely enough, was ignored by parodists until recently when E. B. White not only acknowledged that Walden was a witty book itself, but also placed its somewhat stiff-necked style in comic perspective. Mark Twain grouped Emerson with other New England writers in his notorious burlesque and *faux pas* delivered at the dinner given for Whittier's birthday anniversary. Twain is, of course, a mainstay for the collector of literary satire, as the present volume illustrates. His essay on Cooper could not be omitted, though I have edited it somewhat for my purposes, nor could one reasonably exclude his deflationary essay on Ben Franklin and his bag of prudential maxims. Cooper gained one form of im-

18

mortality through the efforts of Twain, Bret Harte, and Thackeray. In their parodies and burlesques of the Leatherstocking tales Cooper's heavy, periphrastic language, his noble savages and nobler scouts, his fainting females and miracles of woodcraft are made into rare sport for caricature.

The only other American writer who seemed to require a chapter to himself is Henry James whose famous "late manner" became the perfect instrument for parody. When *The American Scene* was published in 1907, many reviewers could find no words to describe their feelings short of burlesquing the intricacies of the style. Throughout his career James was the unwilling recipient of everything from antagonism to ridicule for the elaborate circulocutions and ambiguities of his method. Brother William labored to understand "the gleams and innuendoes and verbal insinuations" of Henry's prose, H. G. Wells compared him to a hippopotamus striving to pick up a pea in the corner of his den, and Frank Colby described the *double-entrendres* of his meaning in a witty satire called "In Darkest James." J. K. Bangs, editor of *Puck* and other humorous magazines in the eighties and nineties, poked fun at the soporific effect of James's endless sentences in "The Return of the Screw." James Thurber has written one of the most skillful of recent parodies of the James style. One sentence from his "The Beast in the Dingle," for instance, is a choice parody of the Jamesian dialogue:

"Let me," it was as though she softly unwrapped it for him, "save you." It needed nothing more to bring him out of it, to bring him, indeed, whole, so to say, hog into it.

Despite its familiarity, Max Beerbohm's brilliant "The Mote in the Middle Distance" has to be included in any consideration of James parodies. Here in a condensed story are all the elements of the James novel: the precocious children, the broken sentences and half-uttered perplexities, the dark hints, and even the final ethical elevation and romantic resignation as the children forego the pleasure of their Christmas stockings. As Keith puts it, "One doesn't even peer!"

The sentimental school of novelists is parodied by Corey Ford's deliciously impudent "The Norris Plan," while Donald Ogden Stewart's "How Love Came to General Grant" is the final word on Harold Bell Wright heroics. Frank Norris took off some of the popular books of the Age of Innocence, including Stephen Crane, Bret Harte, and Richard Harding Davis. Parody found a highly congenial atmosphere in the twenties during which many of the best American exponents of the art did their work. Corey Ford, Louis Untermeyer, Frank Sullivan, Donald Ogden Stewart, and Robert Benchley managed to take off most of the popular writers of that era from Fitzgerald to O'Neill. In the thirties the *New Yorker* carried on the tradition with many fine parodies by Thurber, Wolcott Gibbs, Clifton Fadiman, Cornelia Otis Skinner and others who were able to see the funny side of the hard-boiled school of fiction and the Lost Generation. Finally, the modern cults in verse have been a target for parodists. The impressionists, the imagists, the T. S. Eliot-Ezra Pound ilk, Sandburg, Frost, Lindsay, and Robinson, not to forget Edgar Guest, have received the burlesque touch from such parodists as J. C. Squire, Witter Bynner, Margaret Widdemer, Gilbert Highet, Samuel Hoffenstein, Louis Untermeyer, and John A. Clark.

Among all this parody literature it has been a constant challenge to single out the good parodies from the mediocre, to distinguish the clever from the average. The older pieces were most difficult to select, and I have relied upon those which have best stood the test of time—a most severe test, indeed, in the realm of humor where changing taste is often a cruel judge. The more recent parodies stand more easily by themselves and are more naturally suited to contemporary tastes. But the final judgment of parody must be a subjective one. It is for the reader to decide whether they meet the main requirement—to brighten up the subject, illuminate the original, and provide a happy gleam of recognition or flash of acknowledgment.

It has seemed best not to be too precise in defining the limits of parody. No doubt it is different from its cousins, literary satire, burlesque, and straight imitation. Yet I would hesitate to be the one to draw the lines. Frequently I have found things funnier and more to my purpose in the half-way state. Sometimes the full-blown or deliberate parody is clumsy and obvious where the marginal one is skillful. Mark Twain's essay on Cooper is a borderline case as parody, but it hits the mark. Such parody-essays as E. B. White's "The Retort Transcendental" or Frank Colby's "In Darkest James" or even Henry James's burlesque caricature of that peculiarly American species, the female feminist, are much superior to, say, Bayard Taylor's rather academic exercises in *Diversions of the Echo Club,* though the latter are closer to pure parody.

Here then is my unprecise definition of good parody: *A deflationary piece of matter and impertinency, in prose or verse, of brief duration which satirizes a literary style, personality or mannerism and provides the reader with a quiet explosion of mirth.*

RPF

CHAPTER ONE

Poor Richard In Our Time

"Nowadays a boy cannot follow out a single natural instinct without tumbling over some of those ever-lasting aphorisms. And that boy is hounded to death and robbed of his natural rest, because Franklin said in one of his inspired flights of malignity: 'early to bed and early to rise makes a man healthy, wealthy, and wise.'"

MARK TWAIN

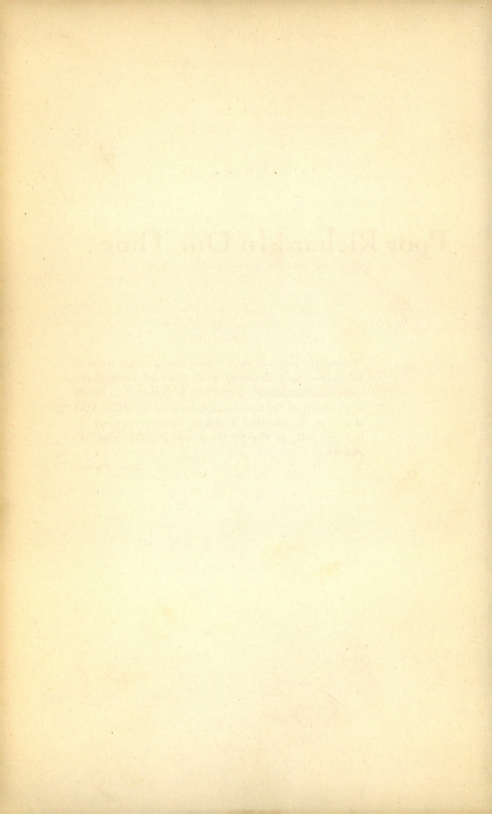

Benjamin Franklin, good old Ben,
Didn't you ever, now and then,
Squander tuppence at the corner bar,
Or shoot a whole shilling for a good cigar?
Benjamin, surely it can't be true
That wisdom and thrift were the whole of you?

Benjamin, were you alive today
Would you always labor and never play?
Would you utter poor richards through serious lips,
And have no time for the comic strips?
And, Ben, would it be your proudest boast
That you founded the Saturday Evening Post?

Benjamin Franklin, it's a shame
To have you cooped in the Hall of Fame,
Chained to a pedestal cold and damp,
And your face on a one-cent postage stamp!
Or else embalmed in a thrift-week ad—
Surely you couldn't have been that bad!

Benjamin Franklin, sober Ben—
The things we do to our famous men!
We raise them up from the merest clods,
And make them impossible demigods.
So I'm keeping your birthday, Ben, today,
In a totally flippant and useless way!

STODDARD KING

("Never put off till tomorrow what you can do the day after tomorrow just as well."—B.F.)

This party was one of those persons whom they call Philosophers. He was twins, being born simultaneously in two different houses in the city of Boston. These houses remain unto this day, and have signs upon them worded in accordance with the facts. The signs are considered well enough to have, though not necessary, because the inhabitants point out the two birthplaces to the stranger anyhow, and sometimes as often as several times in the same day. The subject of this memoir was of a vicious disposition, and early prostituted his talents to the invention of maxims and aphorisms calculated to inflict suffering upon the rising generation of all subsequent ages. His simplest acts, also, were contrived with a view to their being held up for the emulation of boys forever—boys who might otherwise have been happy. It was in this spirit that he became the son of a soap-boiler, and probably for no other reason than that the efforts of all future boys who tried to be anything might be looked upon with suspicion unless they were the sons of soap-boilers. With a malevolence which is without parallel in history, he would work all day, and then sit up nights, and let on to be studying algebra by the light of a smouldering fire, so that all other boys might have to do that also, or else have Benjamin Franklin thrown up to them. Not satisfied with these proceedings, he had a fashion of living wholly on bread and water, and studying astronomy at meal-time—a thing which has brought affliction to millions of boys since, whose fathers had read Franklin's pernicious biography.

His maxims were full of animosity towards boys. Nowadays a boy cannot follow out a single natural instinct without tumbling over some of those everlasting aphorisms and hearing from Franklin on the spot. If he buys two cents' worth of peanuts, his father says, "Remember what Franklin has said, my son—'A groat a day's a penny a year'"; and the comfort is all gone out of those peanuts. If he wants to spin his top when he has done his work, his father quotes, 'Procrastination is the thief of time.' If he does a virtuous action, he never gets anything for it, because "Virtue is its own reward." And that boy is hounded to death and robbed of his natural rest, because Franklin said once, in one of his inspired flights of malignity:

> Early to bed and early to rise
> Makes a man healthy and wealthy and wise.

As if it were any object to a boy to be healthy and wealthy and wise on such terms. The sorrow that that maxim has cost me, through my parents, experimenting on me with it, tongue cannot tell. The legitimate result is my present state of general debility, indigence, and mental aberration. My parents used to have me up before nine o'clock in the morning sometimes when I was a boy. If they had let me take my natural rest where would I have been now? Keeping store, no doubt, and respected by all.

And what an adroit old adventurer the subject of this memoir was! In order to get a chance to fly his kite on Sunday he used to hang a key on the string and let on to be fishing for lightning. And a guileless public would go home chirping about the "wisdom" and the "genius" of the hoary Sabbath-breaker. If anybody caught him playing "mumble-peg" by himself, after the age of sixty, he would immediately appear to be ciphering out how grass grew—as if it was any of his business. My grandfather knew him well, and he says Franklin was always fixed—always ready. If a body, during his old age, happened on him unexpectedly when he was catching flies, or making mud-pies, or sliding on a cellar door, he would immediately look wise, and rip out a maxim, and walk off with his nose in the air and his cap turned wrong side before, trying to appear absent-minded and eccentric. He was a hard lot.

He invented a stove that would smoke your head off in four hours by the clock. One can see the almost devilish satisfaction he took in it by giving it his name.

He was always proud of telling how he entered Philadelphia for the first time, with nothing in the world but two shillings in his pocket and four rolls of bread under his arm. But really, when you came to examine it critically, it was nothing. Anybody could have done it. . . .

Benjamin Franklin did a great many notable things for his country, and made her young name to be honored in many lands as the mother of such a son. It is not the idea of this memoir to ignore that or cover it up. No; the simple idea of it is to snub those pretentious maxims of his, which he worked up with a great show of originality out of truisms that had become wearisome platitudes as early as the dispersion from Babel; and also to snub his stove, and his military inspirations, his unseemly endeavor to make himself conspicuous when he entered Philadelphia, and his flying kite and fooling away his time in all sorts of such ways when he ought to have been foraging for soap-fat, or constructing candles. I merely desired to do away with somewhat of the prevalent calamitous idea among heads of families that Franklin *acquired* his great genius by working for nothing, studying by moonlight, and getting up in the night instead of waiting till morning like a Christian; and that this program, rigidly inflicted, will make a Franklin of every father's fool. It is time these gentlemen were finding out that these execrable eccentricities of instinct and conduct are only the *evidences* of genius, not the *creators* of it. I wish I had been the father of my parents long enough to make them comprehend this truth, and thus prepare them to let their son have an easier time of it. When I was a child I had to boil soap, notwithstanding my father was wealthy, and I had to get up early and study geometry at breakfast, and peddle my own poetry, and do everything just as Franklin did, in the solemn hope that I would be a Franklin some day. And here I am.

MARK TWAIN

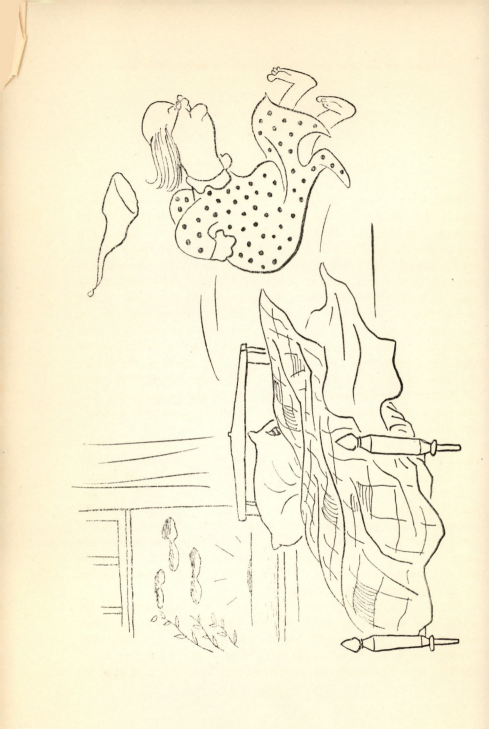

"THE SHRIKE AND THE CHIPMUNKS"

Once upon a time there were two chipmunks, a male and a female. The male chipmunk thought that arranging nuts in artistic patterns was more fun than just piling them up to see how many you could pile up. The female was all for piling up as many as you could. She told her husband that if he gave up making designs with the nuts there would be room in their large cave for a great many more and he would soon become the wealthiest chipmunk in the woods. But he would not let her interfere with his designs, so she flew into a rage and left him. "The shrike will get you," she said, "because you are helpless and cannot look after yourself." To be sure, the female chipmunk had not been gone three nights before the male had to dress for a banquet and could not find his studs or shirt or suspenders. So he couldn't go to the banquet, but that was just as well, because all the chipmunks who did go were attacked and killed by a weasel.

The next day the shrike began hanging around outside the chipmunk's cave, waiting to catch him. The shrike couldn't get in because the doorway was clogged up with soiled laundry and dirty dishes. "He will come out for a walk after breakfast and I will get him then," thought the shrike. But the chipmunk slept all day and did not get up and have breakfast until after dark. Then he came out for a breath of air before beginning to work on a new design. The shrike swooped down to snatch up the chipmunk, but could not see very well on account of the dark, so he batted his head against an alder branch and was killed.

A few days later the female chipmunk returned and saw the awful mess that the house was in. She went to the bed and shook her husband. "What would you do without me?" she demanded. "Just go on living, I guess," he said. "You wouldn't last five days," she told him. She swept the house and did the dishes and sent out

31

the laundry, and then she made the chipmunk get up and wash and dress. "You can't be healthy if you lie in bed all day and never get any exercise," she told him. So she took him for a walk in the bright sunlight and they were both caught and killed by the shrike's brother, a shrike named Stoop.

Moral: Early to rise and early to bed makes a male healthy and wealthy and dead.

JAMES THURBER

("Diligence is the mother of Good Luck, as Poor Richard says, and God gives all things to industry"—B.F.)

"THE PATIENT TOILER WHO GOT IT IN THE USUAL PLACE"

Once there was an Office Employee with a Copy-Book Education. He believed it was his Duty to learn to Labor and to Wait.

He read Pamphlets and Magazine Articles on Success and how to make it a Cinch. He knew that if he made no Changes and never beefed for more Salary, but just buckled down and put in Extra Time and pulled for the House, he would Arrive in time.

The Faithful Worker wanted to be Department Manager. The Hours were short and the Salary large and the Work easy.

He plugged on for many Moons, keeping his Eye on that Roll-Top Desk, for the Manager was getting into the Has-Been Division and he knew that there would be a Vacancy.

At last the House gave the old Manager the Privilege of retiring and living on whatever he had saved.

"Ah, this is where Humble Merit gets its Reward," said the Patient Toiler. "I can see myself counting Money."

That very Day the Main Gazooks led into the Office one of the handsomest Tennis Players that ever worked on Long Island and introduced him all around as the new Department Manager.

"I shall expect you to tell Archibald all about the Business," said the Main Gazooks to the Patient Toiler. "You see he has just graduated from Yale and he doesn't know a dum Thing about Managing anything except a Cat-Boat, but his Father is one of our principal Stock-Holders and he is engaged to a Young Woman whose Uncle is at the head of the Trust."

"I had been hoping to get this Job for myself," said the Faithful Worker, faintly.

"You are so valuable as a Subordinate and have shown such an Aptitude for Detail Work that it would be a Shame to waste you on a $5,000 Job," said the Main Gazooks. "Besides you are not

Equipped. You have not been to Yale. Your Father is not a Stock-Holder. You are not engaged to a Trust. Get back to your High Stool and whatever Archibald wants to know, you tell him."

Moral: One who wishes to be a Figure-Head should not Over-train.

GEORGE ADE

"WISE SAWS AND MODERN INSTANCES, OR POOR RICHARD IN REVERSE"

Saw, *n. A* trite popular saying, or proverb. (Figurative and colloquial.) So called because it makes its way into a wooden head. Following are examples of old saws fitted with new teeth.

A penny saved is a penny to squander.
A man is known by the company that he organizes.
A bad workman quarrels with the man who calls him that.
A bird in the hand is worth what it will bring.
Better late than before anybody has invited you.
Example is better than following it.
Half a loaf is better than a whole one if there is much else.
Think twice before you speak to a friend in need.
What is worth doing is worth the trouble of asking somebody to do it.
Least said is soonest disavowed.
He laughs best who laughs least.
Speak of the Devil and he will hear about it.
Of two evils choose to be the least.
Strike while your employer has a big contract.
Where there's a will there's a won't.

AMBROSE BIERCE

CHAPTER TWO

Leatherstocking In Motley

"His Indians, with proper respect be it said,
Are just Natty Bumppo daubed over with red . . .
And the women he draws from one model don't vary,
All sappy as maples and flat as a prairie."

LOWELL

"Fenimore, lying in his Louis Quatorze hotel in Paris,
passionately musing about Natty Bumppo and the
pathless forest, and mixing his imagination with the
cupids and butterflies on the painted ceiling, while
Mrs. Cooper was struggling with her latest gown in
the next room, and the *dejeuner* was with the countess
at eleven."

D. H. LAWRENCE

"COOPER'S DEFECTS"

Cooper's art has some defects. In one place in *Deerslayer,* and in the restricted space of two-thirds of a page, Cooper has scored 114 offenses against literary art out of a possible 115. It breaks the record.

There are nineteen rules governing literary art in the domain of romantic fiction—some say twenty-two. In *Deerslayer* Cooper violated eighteen of them. . . .

They require that the personages in a tale shall be alive, except in the case of corpses, and that always the reader shall be able to tell the corpses from the others. But this detail has often been overlooked in the *Deerslayer* tale.

MARK TWAIN

[The rules of art] require that when the personages of a tale deal in conversation, the talk shall sound like human talk, and be talk such as human beings would be likely to talk in the given circumstances, and have a discoverable meaning, also a discoverable purpose, and a show of relevancy, and remain in the neighborhood of the subject in hand, and be interesting to the reader, and help out the tale, and stop when the people cannot think of anything more to say. But this requirement has been ignored from the beginning of the *Deerslayer* tale to the end of it.

They require that when the author describes the character of a personage in his tale, the conduct and conversation of that personage shall justify said description. But this law gets little or no attention in the *Deerslayer* tale, as Natty Bumppo's case will amply prove.

They require that when a personage talks like an illustrated, gilt-edged, tree-calf, hand-tooled, seven-dollar Friendship's Offering in the beginning of a paragraph, he shall not talk like a negro minstrel in the end of it. . . .

For instance, when someone asks Deerslayer if he has a sweetheart, and, if so, where she abides, this is his majestic answer:

"She's in the forest—hanging from the boughs of the trees, in a soft rain —in the dew on the open grass—the clouds that float about in the blue heavens—the birds that sing in the woods—the sweet springs where I slake my thirst—and in all other glorious gifts that come from God's Providence!"

And he preceded that, a little before, with this:

" 'It consarns me as all things that touches a fri'nd consarns a fri'nd."

In his little box of stage-properties [Cooper] kept six or eight
cunning devices, tricks, artifices for his savages and woodsmen to
deceive and circumvent each other with, and he was never so happy
as when he was working these innocent things and seeing them go.
A favorite one was to make a moccasined person tread in the tracks
of the moccasined enemy, and thus hide his own trail. Cooper
wore out barrels and barrels of moccasins in working that trick.
Another stage property that he pulled out of his box pretty frequently was his broken twig. He prized his broken twig above all
the rest of his effects, and worked it the hardest. It is a restful
chapter in any book of his when somebody doesn't step on a dry
twig and alarm all the reds and whites for two hundred yards
around. Every time a Cooper person is in peril, and absolute
silence is worth four dollars a minute, he is sure to step on a dry
twig. There may be a hundred handier things to step on, but that
wouldn't satisfy Cooper. Cooper requires him to turn out and find
a dry twig; and if he can't do it, go and borrow one. In fact, the
Leatherstocking Series ought to have been called the Broken Twig
Series. . . .

MARK TWAIN

Now in one place he loses some "females"— as he always calls women—in the edge of a wood near a plain at night in a fog, on purpose to give Bumppo a chance to show off the delicate art of the forest before the reader. These mislaid people are hunting for a fort. They hear a cannon-blast, and a cannon-ball presently comes rolling into the wood and stops at their feet. To the females this suggests nothing. The case is very different with the admirable Bumppo. I wish I may never know peace again if he doesn't strike out promptly and *follow the track* of that cannon-ball across the plain through the dense fog and find the fort. Isn't it a daisy? If Cooper had any real knowledge of Nature's ways of doing things, he had a most delicate art in concealing the fact. For instance: one of his Indian experts, Chingachgook (pronounced Chicago, I think), has lost the trail of a person he is tracking through the forest. Apparently that trail is hopelessly lost. Neither you nor I could ever have guessed out the way to find it. It was very different with Chicago. Chicago was not stumped for long. He turned a running stream out of its course, and there, in the slush of its old bed, were that person's moccasin-tracks. The current did not wash them away, as it would have done in all other like cases—no, even the eternal laws of Nature have to vacate when Cooper wants to put up a delicate job of woodcraft on the reader.

MARK TWAIN

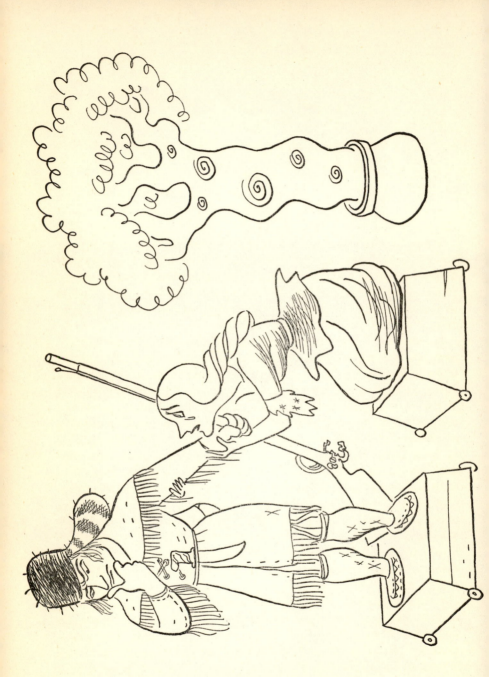

A MODERN INDIAN NOVEL AFTER COOPER"

Chapter I

It was toward the close of a bright October day. The last rays of the setting sun were reflected from one of those sylvan lakes peculiar to the Sierras of California. On the right the curling smoke of an Indian village rose between the columns of the lofty pines, while to the left the log cottage of Judge Tompkins, embowered in buckeyes, completed the enchanting picture.

Although the exterior of the cottage was humble and unpretentious, and in keeping with the wildness of the landscape, its interior gave evidence of the cultivation and refinement of its inmates. An aquarium, containing goldfishes, stood on a marble centre-table at one end of the apartment, while a magnificent grand piano occupied the other. The floor was covered with a yielding tapestry carpet, and the walls were adorned with paintings from the pencils of Van Dyke, Rubens, Tintoretto, Michael Angelo, and the productions of the more modern Turner, Kensett, Church, and Bierstadt. Although Judge Tompkins had chosen the frontiers of civilization as his home, it was impossible for him to entirely forego the habits and tastes of his former life. He was seated in a luxurious armchair, writing at a mahogany *écritoire,* while his daughter, a lovely young girl of seventeen summers, plied her crochet-needle on an ottoman beside him. A bright fire of pine logs flickered and flamed on the ample hearth.

Genevra Octavia Tompkins was Judge Tompkin's only child. Her mother had long since died on the Plains. Reared in affluence, no pains had been spared with the daughter's education. She was a graduate of one of the principal seminaries, and spoke French with a perfect Benicia accent. Peerlessly beautiful, she was dressed in a white *moire antique* robe trimmed with *tulle*. That simple rosebud, with which most heroines exclusively decorate their hair, was all she wore in her raven locks.

The Judge was the first to break the silence.

"Genevra, the logs which compose yonder fire seem to have been incautiously chosen. The sibilation produced by the sap, which exudes copiously therefrom, is not conducive to composition."

"True, father, but I thought it would be preferable to the constant crepitation which is apt to attend the combustion of more seasoned ligneous fragments."

The Judge looked admiringly at the intellectual features of the graceful girl, and half forgot the slight annoyances of the green wood in the musical accents of his daughter. He was smoothing her hair tenderly, when the shadow of a tall figure, which suddenly darkened the doorway, caused him to look up.

Chapter II

It needed but a glance at the new-comer to detect at once the form and features of the haughty aborigine—the untaught and untrammelled son of the forest. Over one shoulder a blanket, negligently but gracefully thrown, disclosed a bare and powerful breast, decorated with a quantity of three-cent postage-stamps which he had despoiled from an Overland Mail stage a few weeks previously. A cast-off beaver of Judge Tompkin's, adorned by a simple feather, covered his erect head, from beneath which his straight locks descended. His right hand hung lightly by his side, while his left was engaged in holding on a pair of pantaloons, which the lawless grace and freedom of his lower limbs evidently could not brook.

"Why," said the Indian, in a low sweet tone,—"why does the Pale Face still follow the track of the Red Man? Why does he pursue him, even as *O-kee-chow,* the wild-cat, chases *Ka-ka,* the skunk? Why are the feet of *Sorrel-top,* the white chief, among the acorns of *Muck-a-Muck,* the mountain forest? Why," he repeated, quietly but firmly abstracting a silver spoon from the table,—"why do you seek to drive him from the wigwams of his fathers? His brothers are already gone to the happy hunting-grounds. Will the Pale Face seek him there?" And, averting his face from the Judge, he hastily slipped a silver cake-basket beneath his blanket, to conceal his emotion.

"*Muck-a-Muck* has spoken," said Genevra, softly. "Let him now listen. Are the acorns of the mountain sweeter than the esculent and nutritious bean of the Pale Face miner? Does my brother prize the edible qualities of the snail above that of the crisp and oleaginous bacon? Delicious are the grasshoppers that sport on the hillside,—are they better than the dried apples of the Pale Faces? Pleasant is the gurgle of the torrent, *Kish-Kish,* but is it better than the cluck-cluck of old Bourbon from the old stone bottle?"

"Ugh!" said the Indian,—"ugh! good. The White Rabbit is wise. Her words fall as the snow on Tootoonolo, and the rocky heart of Muck-a-Muck is hidden. What says my brother the Gray Gopher of Dutch Flat?"

"She has spoken, Muck-a-Muck," said the Judge, gazing fondly on his daughter. "It is well. Our treaty is concluded. No, thank you,—you need *not* dance the Dance of Snow Shoes, or the Moccasin Dance, the Dance of Green Corn, or the Treaty Dance. I would be alone. A strange sadness overpowers me."

"I go," said the Indian. "Tell your great chief in Washington, the Sachem Andy, that the Red Man is retiring before the footsteps of the adventurous Pioneer. Inform him, if you please, that westward the star of empire takes its way, that the chiefs of the Pi-Ute nation are for Reconstruction to a man, and that Klamath will poll a heavy Republican vote in the fall."

And folding his blanket more tightly around him, Muck-a-Muck withdrew.

Chapter III

GENEVRA TOMPKINS stood at the door of the log-cabin, looking after the retreating Overland Mail stage which conveyed her father to Virginia City. "He may never return again," sighed the young girl as she glanced at the frightfully rolling vehicle and wildly careering horses,—"at least, with unbroken bones. Should he meet with an accident! I mind me now a fearful legend, familiar to my childhood. Can it be that the drivers on this line are privately instructed to despatch all passengers maimed by accident, to prevent tedious litigation? No, no. But why this weight upon my heart?"

She seated herself at the piano and lightly passed her hand over the keys. Then, in a clear mezzo-soprano voice, she sang the first verse of one of the most popular Irish ballads:—

"O Arrah, my dheelish, the distant dudheen
Lies soft in the moonlight, ma bouchal vourneen:
The springing gossoons on the heather are still,
And the caubeens and colleens are heard on the hills."

But as the ravishing notes of her sweet voice died upon the air, her hands sank listlessly to her side. Music could not chase away the mysterious shadow from her heart. Again she rose. Putting on a white crape bonnet, and carefully drawing a pair of lemon-colored gloves over her taper fingers, she seized her parasol and plunged into the depths of the pine forest.

Chapter IV

GENEVRA had not proceeded many miles before a weariness seized upon her fragile limbs, and she would fain seat herself upon the trunk of a prostrate pine, which she previously dusted with her handkerchief. The sun was just sinking below the horizon, and the scene was one of gorgeous and sylvan beauty. "How beautiful is Nature!" murmured the innocent girl, as, reclining gracefully against the root of the tree, she gathered up her skirts and tied a handkerchief around her throat. But a low growl interrupted her meditation. Starting to her feet, her eyes met a sight which froze her blood with terror.

The only outlet to the forest was the narrow path, barely wide enough for a single person, hemmed in by trees and rocks, which she had just traversed. Down this path, in Indian file, came a monstrous grizzly, followed by a California lion, a wild-cat, and a buffalo, the rear being brought up by a wild Spanish bull. The mouths of the first three animals were distended with frightful significance; the horns of the last were lowered as ominously. As Genevra was preparing to faint, she heard a low voice behind her.

"Eternally dog-gone my skin ef this ain't the puttiest chance yet."

At the same moment, a long, shining barrel dropped lightly from behind her, and rested over her shoulder.

Genevra shuddered.

"Dern ye—don't move!"

Genevra became motionless.

The crack of a rifle rang through the woods. Three frightful yells were heard, and two sullen roars. Five animals bounded into the air and five lifeless bodies lay upon the plain. The well-aimed bullet had done its work. Entering the open throat of the grizzly, it had traversed his body only to enter the throat of the California lion, and in like manner the catamount, until it passed through into the respective foreheads of the bull and the buffalo, and finally fell flattened from the rocky hillside.

Genevra turned quickly. "My preserver!" she shrieked, and fell into the arms of Natty Bumpo, the celebrated Pike Ranger of Donner Lake.

Chapter V

The moon rose cheerfully above Donner Lake. On its placid bosom a dug-out canoe glided rapidly, containing Natty Bumpo and Genevra Tompkins.

Both were silent. The same thought possessed each, and perhaps there was sweet companionship even in the unbroken quiet. Genevra bit the handle of her parasol and blushed. Natty Bumpo took a fresh chew of tobacco. At length Genevra said, as if in half-spoken revery:—

"The soft shining of the moon and the peaceful ripple of the waves seem to say to us various things of an instructive and moral tendency."

"You may bet yer pile on that, Miss," said her companion, gravely. "It's all the preachin' and psalm-singin' I've heern since I was a boy."

"Noble being!" said Miss Tompkins to herself, glancing at the stately Pike as he bent over his paddle to conceal his emotion. "Reared in this wild seclusion, yet he has become penetrated with visible consciousness of a Great First Cause." Then, collecting herself, she said aloud: "Methinks 't were pleasant to glide ever thus down the stream of life, hand in hand with the one being whom the soul claims as its affinity. But what am I saying?"—and the delicate-minded girl hid her face in her hands.

A long silence ensued, which was at length broken by her companion.

"Ef you mean you're on the marry," he said, thoughtfully, "I ain't in no wise partikler!"

"My husband," faltered the blushing girl; and she fell into his arms.

In ten minutes more the loving couple had landed at Judge Tompkins's.

Chapter VI

A YEAR has passed away. Natty Bumpo was returning from Gold Hill, where he had been to purchase provisions. On his way to Donner Lake, rumors of an Indian uprising met his ears. "Dern their pesky skins, ef they dare to touch my Jenny," he muttered between his clenched teeth.

It was dark when he reached the borders of the lake. Around a glittering fire he dimly discerned dusky figures dancing. They were in war paint. Conspicuous among them was the renowned Muck-a-Muck. But why did the fingers of Natty Bumpo tighten convulsively around his rifle?

The chief held in his hand long tufts of raven hair. The heart of the pioneer sickened as he recognized the clustering curls of Genevra. In a moment his rifle was at his shoulder, and with a sharp "ping," Muck-a-Muck leaped into the air a corpse. To knock out the brains of the remaining savages, tear the tresses from the stiffening hand of Muck-a-Muck, and dash rapidly forward to the cottage of Judge Tompkins, was the work of a moment.

He burst open the door. Why did he stand transfixed with open mouth and distended eyeballs? Was the sight too horrible to be borne? On the contrary, before him, in her peerless beauty, stood Genevra Tompkins, leaning on her father's arm.

"Ye'r not scalped, then!" gasped her lover.

"No. I have no hesitation in saying that I am not; but why this abruptness?" responded Genevra.

Bumpo could not speak, but frantically produced the silken tresses. Genevra turned her face aside.

"Why, that's her waterfall!" said the Judge.

Bumpo sank fainting to the floor.

The famous Pike chieftain never recovered from the deceit, and refused to marry Genevra, who died, twenty years afterwards, of a broken heart. Judge Tompkins lost his fortune in Wild Cat. The stage passes twice a week the deserted cottage at Donner Lake. Thus was the death of Muck-a-Muck avenged.

BRET HARTE

I.

The King of France was walking on the terrace of Versailles; the fairest, not only of Queens, but of women, hung fondly on the Royal arm; while the children of France were indulging in their infantile hilarity in the alleys of the magnificent garden of Le Notre (from which Niblo's garden has been copied in our own Empire city of New Cork), and playing at leap-frog with their uncle, the Count of Provence; gaudy courtiers, emblazoned with orders, glittered in the groves, and murmured frivolous talk in the ears of high-bred beauty.

"Marie, my beloved," said the ruler of France, taking out his watch, "'tis time that the Minister of America should be here."

"Your Majesty should know the time," replied Marie Antoinette, archly, and in an Austrian accent; "is not my Royal Louis the first watchmaker in his empire?"

The King cast a pleased glance at his repeater, and kissed with courtly grace the fair hand of her who had made him the compliment. "My Lord Bishop of Autun," said he to Monsieur de Tallyrand Périgord, who followed the royal pair, in his quality of arch-chamberlain of the empire, "I pray you look through the gardens, and tell his Excellency Doctor Franklin that the King waits." The Bishop ran off, with more than youthful agility, to seek the United States Minister. "These Republicans," he added, confidentially, and with something of a supercilious look, "are but rude courtiers, methinks."

"Nay," interposed the lovely Antoinette, "rude courtiers, Sire, they may be; but the world boasts not of more accomplished gentlemen. I have seen no grandee of Versailles that has the noble bearing of this American envoy and his suite. They have the refinement of the Old World, with all the simple elegance of the New. Though they have perfect dignity of manner, they have an engaging modesty which I have never seen equalled by the best of the proud English nobles with whom they wage war. I am told they speak their very language with a grace which the haughty Islanders who oppress them never attained. They are independent, yet never insolent; elegant, yet always respectful; and brave, but not in the least boastful."

"What! savages and all, Marie?" exclaimed Louis, laughing, and chucking the lovely Queen playfully under the royal chin. "But here comes Doctor Franklin, and your friend the Cacique with him." In fact, as the monarch spoke, the Minister of the United States made his appearance, followed by a gigantic warrior in the garb of his native woods.

Knowing his place as Minister of a sovereign state (yielding even then in dignity to none, as it surpasses all now in dignity, in valor, in honesty, in strength, and civilization,) the Doctor nodded to the Queen of France, but kept his hat on as he faced the French monarch, and did not cease whittling the cane he carried in his hand.

"I was waiting for you, sir," the King said, peevishly, in spite of the alarmed pressure which the Queen gave his royal arm.

"The business of the Republic, Sire, must take precedence even of your Majesty's wishes," replied Dr. Franklin. "When I was a poor printer's boy and ran errands, no lad could be more punctual than poor Ben Franklin; but all other things must yield to the service of the United States of North America. I have done. What would you, Sire?" and the intrepid republican eyed the monarch with a serene and easy dignity, which made the descendent of St. Louis feel ill at ease.

"I wished to—to say farewell to Tatua before his departure," said Louis XVI, looking rather awkward. "Approach, Tatua." And the gigantic Indian strode up, and stood undaunted before the first magistrate of the French nation: again the feeble monarch quailed before the terrible simplicity of the glance of the denizen of the primaeval forests.

The redoubted chief of the Nose-ring Indians was decorated in his warpaint, and in his top-knot was a peacock's feather, which had been given him out of the head-dress of the beautiful Princess of Lamballe. His nose, from which hung the ornament from which his ferocious tribe took its designation, was painted a light-blue, a circle of green and orange was drawn round each eye, while serpentine stripes of black, white, and vermilion alternately were smeared on his forehead, and descended over his cheek-bones to his chin. His manly chest was similarly tattooed and painted, and round his brawny neck and arms hung innumerable bracelets and necklaces of human teeth, extracted (one only from each skull) from the jaws of those who had fallen by the terrible tomahawk at his girdle. His moccasins, and his blanket, which was draped on his arm and fell in picturesque folds to his feet, were fringed with tufts of hair—the black, the gray, the auburn, the golden ringlet of beauty, the red lock from the forehead of the Scottish or the Northern soldier, the snowy tress of extreme old age, the flaxon down of infancy—all were there, dreadful reminiscences of the chief's triumphs in war. The warrior leaned on his enormous rifle, and faced the King.

"And it was with that carabine that you shot Wolfe in '57?" said Louis, eyeing the warrior and his weapon. " 'Tis a clumsy lock, and methinks I could mend it," he added mentally.

"The chief of the French pale-faces speaks truth," Tatua said. "Tatua was a boy when he went first on the war-path with Montcalm."

"And shot a Wolfe at the first fire!" said the King.

"The English are braves, though their faces are white," replied the Indian. "Tatua shot the raging Wolfe of the English; but the other wolves caused the foxes to go to earth." A smile played round Dr. Franklin's lips, as he whittled his cane with more vigor than ever.

"I believe, your Excellency, Tatua has done good service elsewhere than at Quebec," the King said, appealing to the American Envoy: "at Bunker's Hill, at Brandywine, at York Island? Now that Lafayette and my brave Frenchmen are among you, your Excellency need have no fear but that the war will finish quickly—yes, yes, it will finish quickly. They will teach you discipline, and the way to conquer."

"King Louis of France," said the Envoy, clapping his hat down over his head, and putting his arms a-kimbo, "we have learned that from the British, to whom we are superior in everything: and I'd have your Majesty to know that in the art of whipping the world we have no need of any French lessons. If your regulars jine General Washington, 'tis to larn from him how Britishers are licked; for I'm blest if yu know the way yet."

Tatua said, "Ugh," and gave a rattle with the butt of his carabine, which made the timid monarch start; the eyes of the lovely Antoinette flashed fire, but it played round the head of the dauntless American Envoy harmless as the lightning which he knew how to conjure away.

The King fumbled in his pocket, and pulled out a Cross of the Order of the Bath. "Your Excellency wears no honor," the monarch said; "but Tatua, who is not a subject, only an ally, of the United States, may. Noble Tatua, I appoint you Knight Companion of my noble Order of the Bath. Wear this cross upon your breast in memory of Louis of France;" and the King held out the decoration to the Chief.

Up to that moment the Chief's countenance had been impassible. No look either of admiration or dislike had appeared upon that grim and war-painted visage. But now, as Louis spoke, Tatua's face assumed a glance of ineffable scorn, as, bending his head, he took the bauble.

"I will give it to one of my squaws," he said. "The papooses in my lodge will play with it. Come, Médecine, Tatua will go and drink fire-water;" and, shouldering his carabine, he turned his broad back without ceremony upon the monarch and his train, and disappeared down one of the walks of the garden. Franklin found him when his own interview with the French Chief Magistrate was over; being attracted to the spot where the Chief was, by the crack of his well-known rifle. He was laughing in his quiet way. He had shot the Colonel of the Swiss Guards through his cockade.

Three days afterwards, as the gallant frigate, the "Repudiator," was sailing out of Brest Harbor, the gigantic form of an Indian might be seen standing on the binnacle in conversation with Commodore Bowie, the commander of the noble ship. It was Tatua, the Chief of the Nose-rings.

II.

Leatherlegs and Tom Coxswain did not accompany Tatua when he went to the Parisian metropolis on a visit to the father of the

French pale-faces. Neither the Legs nor the Sailor cared for the gayety and the crowd of cities; the stout mariner's home was in the puttock-shrouds of the old "Repudiator." The stern and simple trapper loved the sound of the waters better than the jargon of the French of the old country. "I can follow the talk of a Pawnee," he said, "or wag my jaw, if so be necessity bids me to speak, by a Sioux's council-fire; and I can patter Canadian French with the hunters who come for peltries to Nachitoches or Thichimuchimachy; but from the tongue of a Frenchwoman, with white flour on her head, and war-paint on her face, the Lord deliver poor Natty Pumpo."

"Amen and amen!" said Tom Coxswain. "There was a woman in our aft-scuppers when I went a-whalin in the little 'Grampus'— and Lord love you, Pumpo, you poor land-swab, she was as pretty a craft as ever dowsed a tarpauling—there was a woman on board the 'Grampus,' who before we'd struck our first fish, or biled our first blubber, set the whole crew in a mutiny. I mind me of her now, Natty,—her eye was sich a piercer that you could see to steer by it in a Newfoundland fog; her nose stood out like the 'Grampus's' jibboom, and her woice, Lord love you, her woice sings in my ears even now:—it set the Captain a'quarrelin with the Mate, who was hanged in Boston harbor for harpoonin of his officer in Baffin's Bay;—it set me and Bob Bunting a-pouring broadsides into each other's old timbers, whereas me and Bob was worth all the women that ever shipped a hawser. It cost me three years' pay as I'd stowed away for the old mother, and might have cost me ever so much more, only bad luck to me, she went and married a little tailor out of Nantucket; and I've hated women and tailors ever since!" As he spoke, the hardy tar dashed a drop of brine from his tawny cheek, and once more betook himself to splice the taffrail.

Though the brave frigate lay off Havre de Grace, she was not idle. The gallant Bowie and his intrepid crew made repeated descents upon the enemy's seaboard. The coasts of Rutland and merry Leicestershire have still many a legend of fear to tell; and the children of the British fishermen tremble even now when they speak of the terrible "Repudiator." She was the first of the mighty American war-ships that have taught the domineering Briton to respect the valor of the Republic.

The novelist ever and anon finds himself forced to adopt the sterner tone of the historian, when describing deeds connected with his country's triumphs. It is well known that during the two months in which she lay off Havre, the "Repudiator" had brought more prizes into that port than had ever before been seen in the astonished French waters. Her actions with the "Dettingen" and the "Elector" frigates form part of our country's history; their defence—it may be said without prejudice to national vanity—was worthy of Britons and of the audacious foe they had to encounter; and it must be owned, that but for a happy fortune which presided on that day over the destinies of our country, the chance of the combat might have been in favor of the British vessels. It was not until the "Elector" blew up, at a quarter past three P.M., by a lucky shot which fell into her caboose, and communicated with the powder-magazine, that Commodore Bowie was enabled to lay himself on board the "Dettingen," which he carried sword in hand. Even when the American boarders had made their lodgment on the "Dettingen's" binnacle, it is possible that the battle would still have gone against us. The British were still seven to one; their cannonades, loaded with marline-spikes, swept the gun-deck, of which we had possession, and decimated our little force; when a rifle-ball from the shrouds of the "Repudiator" shot Captain Mumford under the star of the Guelphic Order which he wore, and the Americans, with a shout, rushed up the companion to the quarter-deck, upon the astonished foe. Pike and cutlass did the rest of the bloody work. Rumford, the gigantic first-lieutenant of the "Dettingen," was cut down by Commodore Bowie's own sword, as they engaged hand to hand; and it was Tom Coxswain who tore down the British flag, after having slain the Englishman at the wheel. Peace be to the souls of the brave! The combat was honorable alike to the victor and the vanquished; and it never can be said that an American warrior depreciated a gallant foe. The bitterness of defeat was enough to the haughty islanders who had to suffer. The people of Herne Bay were lining the shore, near which the combat took place, and cruel must have been the pang to them when they saw the Stars and Stripes rise over the old flag of the

Union, and the "Dettingen" fall down the river in tow of the Republican frigate.

Another action Bowie contemplated; the boldest and most daring perhaps ever imagined by seamen. It is this which has been so wrongly described by European annalists, and of which the British until now have maintained the most jealous secrecy.

Portsmouth Harbor was badly defended. Our intelligence in that town and arsenal gave us precise knowledge of the disposition of the troops, the forts, and the ships there; and it was determined to strike a blow which should shake the British power in its centre.

That a frigate of the size of the "Repudiator" should enter the harbor unnoticed, or could escape its guns unscathed, passed the notions of even American temerity. But upon the memorable 26th of June, 1782, the "Repudiator" sailed out of Havre Roads in a thick fog, under cover of which she entered and cast anchor in Bonchurch Bay, in the Isle of Wight. To surprise the Martello Tower and take the feeble garrison thereunder, was the work of Tom Coxswain and a few of his blue-jackets. The surprised garrison laid down their arms before him.

It was midnight before the boats of the ship, commanded by Lieutenant Bunker, pulled out from Bonchurch with muffled oars, and in another hour were off the Common Hard of Portsmouth, having passed the challenges of the "Thetis" and the "Amphion" frigates, and the "Polyanthus" brig.

There had been on that day great feasting and merriment on board the Flag-ship lying in the harbor. A banquet had been given in honor of the birthday of one of the princes of the royal line of the Guelphs—the reader knows the propensity of Britons when liquor is in plenty. All on board that royal ship were more or less overcome. The Flag-ship was plunged in a deathlike and drunken sleep. The very officer of the watch was intoxicated: he could not see the "Repudiator's" boats as they shot swiftly through the waters; nor had he time to challenge her seamen as they swarmed up the huge sides of the ship.

At the next moment Tom Coxswain stood at the wheel of the "Royal George"—the Briton who had guarded, a corpse at his feet. The hatches were down. The ship was in possession of the "Repudiator's" crew. They were busy in her rigging, bending her sails to carry her out of the harbor. The well-known heave of the men at the windlass woke up Kempenfelt in his state-cabin. We know, or rather do not know, the result; for who can tell by whom the lower-deck ports of the brave ship were opened, and how the haughty prisoners below sunk the ship and its conquerors rather than yield her as a prize to the Republic!

Only Tom Coxswain escaped of victors and vanquished. His tale was told to his Captain and to Congress, but Washington forbade its publication; and it was but lately that the faithful seaman told it to me, his grandson, on his hundred-and-fifteenth birthday.

WILLIAM MAKEPEACE THACKERAY

"MR. COPYMORE FUMMER, AUTHOR OF THE LEATHER-LEG

NOVELS REFUSES AN INVITATION"

(The excitment over the arrival of Dickens in America in 1842 provoked such a flutter of literary activity and newspaper talk in and around Boston that Samuel Kettell was inspired to publish a lengthy burlesque of the "Boz" dinner under the title, *Quozziana: or Letters from Great Goslington, giving an account of the Quoz Dinner and Other Matters by Sampson Short-and-Fat.* The book consisted of speeches and letters by familiar members of the Young Literati of the day and culminated with the "Quoz" dinner presided over by the President of the Day, Simon Squizzlebrain. Among the letters read to the gathering was the following from Mr. Copymore Fummer, the author of the Leather-leg Novels, who had been invited to the dinner but could not attend.)

Fummington, Jan., 20, 1842

Gentlemen—

The invitation which you have very properly and with great good judgment forwarded to me, respectfully soliciting the honor of my company at the Quoz dinner, is no less honorable to myself than to *your* selves. The author of the Leather-leg Novels would indeed have been astonished, had he been passed without notice on this occasion.

I must, however, decline the invitation. From *me* this would be sufficient without any further explanation of the cause; but my known affability impels me to a disclosure. In fact, it highly interests the whole world of literature to know not only what I *am* doing, but also what I am *not* doing. Be it known, then, that for twenty years past, I have been suffering under the malady of a stiff neck, and a high shirt-collar, so as entirely to disable me from making a civil congee. Public dinners are considered by the common people, as I understand, very agreeable things. I should have, abstractedly, no objection to honor such a *re-union* with my presence, were the assembly composed of the first circles, and imbued with the *ton* of good society; but the rigidity of my jugular muscles seems imcompatible with any heterogeneous collection of individuals.

But though you will be deprived of my company—a calamity indeed to be regretted—I return you my thanks which, I trust, will console you in some measure for the disappointment. Gentlemen, I knew you must be, as men of taste, admirers of the Leatherleg Novels—those admirable fictions, in which I have shown so rich an invention and so boundless a versatility of powers. The Leatherleg Novels are the colossal columns on which rests the whole fabric of our native literature. Any other writer, of feebler powers than myself, would have carried his Leatherlegs through a single tale at most—but I have spun him out through half a dozen. Falstaff made eleven buckram men out of two: I have beaten the fat knight, by making six leather-legged heroes out of *one*. Since the star of my genius, gentlemen, burst on the astonished world, our whole body of literature has gone upon leather legs; and every reader acknowledges that there is "nothing like leather." In fact I may say in the language of Dryden, slightly modified—

> "Leatherlegs the rocks—
> Leatherlegs the streams—
> Leatherlegs the woods and hollow mountains ring."

I will only add for the present, gentlemen, in order that the public may receive additional gratification, that I am now very agreeably occupied in lawsuits. Give my compliments to Mr. Quoz and inform him, and all other persons, that my opinion of my self is still as high as ever.

Yours &c.

COPYMORE FUMMER

CHAPTER THREE

The Deflowering of New England

Verses of great men remind us,
We can also rise and shine,
And departing leave behind us
Mighty platitudes—in rime!
A Slam at Life

"A GARLAND OF IBIDS FOR VAN WYCK BROOKS"[1]

I have just finished reading a book[2] which struck me as being one of the finest books I have read since I read "The Flowering of New England," by the same author.[3] But there is a fly in the ointment. I have been rendered cockeyed by the footnotes. There seem to be too many of them, even for a book largely about Boston.[4] I do not know why the author had to have so many footnotes. Maybe he had a reason for each one, but I suspect the footnote habit has crept up on him, for I got out his book on Emerson,[5] published in 1932, and he used practically no footnotes in it.

You read along in "New England: Indian Summer," interested to the hilt in what Van Wyck Brooks is telling you about Longfellow,[6] Thoreau,[7] Phillips,[8] James,[9] Alcott,[10] Lowell,[11] Adams,[12]

---

1. Or "A Garland of Ibids."

2. "New England: Indian Summer."

3. Van Wyck Brooks, author of "New England: Indian Summer," "The Flowering of New England," "The Life of Emerson," "The Ordeal of Mark Twain," and other books.

4. Sometimes referred to as The Hub. Capital and chief city of Massachusetts. Scene of the Boston Tea Party and the arrest of Henry L. Mencken. Bostonians are traditionally noted for their civic pride, or, as an envious New York critic once termed it, their parochial outlook. It is related that on an occasion when Saltonstall Boylston learned that his friend L. Cabot Lowell was leaving for a trip around the world, he inquired of Lowell, "Which route shall you take, L. C.?" "Oh, I shall go by way of Dedham, of course," replied Mr. Lowell. On another occasion, the old Back Bay aristocrat Ralph Waldo Mulcahy said to Oliver Wendell Rooney, "By the way, Rooney, did your ancestors come over on the Mayflower?" "Oh, no," replied Mr. Rooney. "They arrived on the next boat. They sent the servants over on the May-flower."

5. Ralph Waldo Emerson, Sage of Concord and famous transcendentalist philosopher, not to be confused with Ralph McAllister Ingersoll, editor of PM.

6. Henry Wadsworth Longfellow, Good Gray Poet. Longfellow was no footnote addict. He preferred foot*prints*. Cf. his "Psalm of Life":

> And, departing, leave behind us
> Footprints on the sands of time.

7. Henry David Thoreau, philosopher who lived at Walden Pond for two years on carrots, twigs, nuts, minnows, creek water and, as Margaret Fuller suspected (booming it out at Brook Farm in that full, rich voice of hers, to the dismay of William Ellery Channing, Henry Wadsworth Longfellow, Edward Everett Hale, John Lothrop Mot-

and other great figures of the Periclean Age of the Hub,[13] when suddenly there is a footnote.

The text, is in fine, clear type. The footnotes are in small type. So it is quite a chore to keep focussing up and down the page, especially if you have old eyes or a touch of astigmatism.[14] By and

---

ley, Charles Eliot Norton, and William Lloyd Garrison), sirloin steaks and creamery butter smuggled to him by Emerson. Suffering as he did from a vitamin deficiency, the result of too much moss in his diet, Thoreau became somewhat of a misanthrope and would often creep up behind members of the Saturday Club and shout "Boo!," or, as some authorities maintain, "Pooh!" The matter is not clarified very much, one must admit, by a letter Mrs. Harriet Beecher Stowe wrote to her son, Harriet Beecher Stowe, Jr. (not to be confused with Herbert Bayard Swope), on June 7, 1854, in which she states: "Not much to write home about, as the saying goes. Dave Thoreau here for supper last nite [sic]. He got into an argument with John Greenleaf Whittier, the Good Gray Poet, as to whether snow is really ermine too dear for an earl, and Greenleaf called him a Communist. Dave then crept up behind Greenleaf and shouted either 'Boo!' [sic] or 'Pooh!' [sic], I couldn't make out wich [sic]. All well here except F. Marion Crawford, Sarah Orne Jewett, Charles Dudley Warner, Thomas Wentworth Higginson, and William Dean Howells, who complain of feeling sic [sic]. Your aff. mother, H. B. Stowe, Sr."

8. Wendell Phillips. He was about the only Bostonian of his time who wore no middle name and he was therefore considered half naked. Even Mark Twain, when he went to visit Howells in Boston, registered as Samuel Langhorne Clemens.

9. Probably not Jesse James. Probably is either William James, deviser of Pragmatic Sanctions, or his brother Henry, the novelist. It was about this time that Henry James was going through his transition period, and could not make up his mind whether he was in England living in America or in America living in England.

10. Amos Bronson Alcott, educator and bad provider. The Mr. Micawber of his day. Not to be confused with Novelist Bus Bronson of Yale or Mrs. Chauncey Olcott.

11. James Russell Lowell, poet, essayist, and kinfolk of late rotund, cigar-smoking Back Bay Poetess Amy Lowell, no rhymester she.

12. Henry Adams, author of "The Education of Henry Adams," by Henry Adams. Not to be confused with Henry Adams, Samuel Adams, John Adams, John Quincy Adams, Abigail Adams, Charles Edward Adams (not to be confused with Charles Francis Adams, Charles Henry Adams, or Henry Adams), Maude Adams, Franklin Pierce Adams, Samuel Hopkins Adams, Bristow Adams, George Matthew Adams, James Truslow Adams, Adams Express, Adams & Flanagan, Horace Flanagan, or Louis Adamic.

13. Sometimes referred to as Boston. One is reminded of the famous quatrain:

> Here's to the City of Boston,
> The home of Filene and the Card.,
> Where the Rileys speak only to Cabots
> And the Cabots speak only to God!

14. In this connection, it is interesting to note that Louisa May Alcott had a touch of astigmatism, if we are to accept the word of Charles Eliot Norton. Edward Everett Hale states in his Letters, Vol. XV, Ch. 8, pp. 297 *et seq.*, that William Cullen Bryant told Oliver Wendell Holmes that on one occasion when the fun was running high at Thomas Wentworth Higginson's home and all barriers were down, Thomas Bailey Aldrich had put the question bluntly to Charles Eliot Norton, saying, "Now listen, has Louisa May Alcott got astigmatism or hasn't she?" Charles Eliot Norton answered, perhaps unwisely, "Yes." Cf. the famous dictum of General William Tecumseh Sherman, sometimes erroneously ascribed to General Ulysses Simpson Grant: "Never bring up a lady's name in the mess."

by you say to yourself, "I be damn if I look down at any more foot-notes!" But you do, because the book is so interesting you don't want to miss even the footnotes.[15]

When you get to the footnote at the bottom of the page, like as not all you find is *ibid*. *Ibid* is a great favorite of footnote-mad authors.[16] It was a great favorite with Gibbon.[17] How come writers of fiction do not need footnotes? Take Edna Ferber.[18] She doesn't use footnotes. Suppose Edna Herford[19] took to writing her novels in this manner: "Cicely Ticklepaw* sat at her dressing table in a brown study. She had 'a very strange feeling she'd ne'er felt before, a kind of a grind of depression.'† Could it be love?‡ If so, why had she sent him§ away? She sighed, and a soft cry of 'Aye me!'‖ escaped her. Seizing a nail file desperately, she commenced hacking away at her fingernails, when a voice behind her said, 'Oh! that I were a glove upon that hand, that I might touch that cheek!'$ Cicely reddened, turned. It was Cleon Bel Murphy! Softly, she told him, 'What man art thou, that, thus bescreen'd in night, so stumblest on my counsel?' "&

---

15. Ah there, Van Wyck!

16. So is cf.

17. Edward Gibbon, English historian, not to be confused with Cedric Gibbons, Hollywood art director. Edward Gibbon was a great hand for footnotes, especially if they gave him a chance to show off his Latin. He would come sniffing up to a nice, spicy morsel of scandal about the Romans and then, just as the reader expected him to dish the dirt, he'd go into his Latin routine, somewhat as follows: "In those days vice reached depths not plumbed since the reign of Caligula and it was an open secret that the notorious Empress Theodoro in *tres partes divisa erat* and that she was also addicted to the *argumentum ad hominem!*" Gibbon, prissy little fat man that he was, did that just to tease readers who had flunked Caesar.

18. Edna Cabot Ferber, contemporary New England novelist. It is related of Edna Ferber that she once met Oliver Herford in Gramercy Park and recoiled at the sight of an extremely loud necktie he was wearing. "Heavens above, Oliver Herford!" exclaimed Miss Ferber, never one not to speak her mind. "That is a terrible cravat. Why do you wear it?" "Because it is my wife's whim that I wear it," explained Oliver Herford. "Well, land sakes alive, before I'd wear a tie like that just on account of a wife's whim!" jeered Miss Ferber. "You don't know my wife," said Oliver Herford. "She's got a whim of iron." Miss Ferber later made this incident the basis for the dramatic battle between the husband and wife in her novel "The Cravat."

19. No, no, no, not Edna Herford! Edna *Ferber*: Edna Herford is the fellow who had the wife with the iron whim.

* Blonde, lovely, and twenty-one.

† See "I'm Falling in Love with Someone"—Victor Herbert.

‡ Sure

§ Cleon Bel Murphy, the man she loves.

‖ "Romeo and Juliet," Act II, Scene 2.

$ *Ibid.*

& *Ibid.*

What would Van Wyck Brooks say if Edna Ferber wrote like that?[20] Yes. Exactly. Now, where were we?[21] No, I was not. I know what I was saying. You keep out of this. You're a footnote.[22] Yeah? Well, just for that, no more footnotes. Out you go![23] I am, that's who.[24] See what I mean, Van Wyck? Give a footnote an inch and it'll take a foot.[25] I give up. They got me. And they'll get you too in the end, Van Wyck. You may think you're strong enough to keep 'em under control; you may think you can take a footnote or leave it. All I say is, remember Dr. Jekyll! Lay off 'em, Van. I'm telling you for your own good.

UNEASY BROOKS FAN[26]

---

20. And what would Edna Ferber say if Edna Ferber wrote like that?
21. You were saying Louisa May Alcott had astigmatism.
22. Yeah? And how far would you have got in this article without footnotes?
23. Who's gonna put me out?
24. Yeah? You and who else?
25. Yoo-hoo! Footnote!
26. Frank Saltonstall Sullivan.

He slew the noble Mudjekeewis,
With his skin he made them mittens;
Made them with the fur-side inside,
Made them with the skin-side outside;
He, to keep the warm side inside,
Put the cold side, skin-side, outside;
He, to keep the cold side outside,
Put the warm side, fur-side, inside:—
That's why he put the cold side outside,
Why he put the warm side inside,
Why he turned them inside outside.

GEORGE A. STRONG

Just as, to a big umbrella
Is the handle when it's raining,
So a wife is, to her husband;
Though the handle do support it,
'Tis the top keeps all the rain off;
Though the top gets all the wetting,
'Tis the handle bears the burden;
So the top is good for nothing,
If there isn't any handle,
And the case holds vice versa.
In this way, did Milkanwatha
Reason when he was a-thinking,
Thinking of his Pogee-wogee,
Of the blue-eyed Sweet Potato,
In the Village of the Noodles.

Song of Milkanwatha

Do you ask me what I think of
This new song of Hiawatha,
With its legends and traditions,
And its frequent repetitions
Of hard names which make the jaw ache,
And of words most unpoetic?
I should answer, I should tell you
I esteem it wild and wayward,
Slipshod metre, scanty sense,
Honour paid to Mudjekeewis,
But no honour to the muse.

                    J. W. MORRIS

This is the metre Columbian. The soft-flowing trochees and dactyls,
Blended with fragments spondaic, and here and there an iambus,
Syllables often sixteen, or more or less, as it happens,
Difficult always to scan, and depending greatly on accent,
Being a close imitation, in English, of Latin hexameters—
Fluent in sound and avoiding the stiffness of blank verse,
Having the grandeur and flow of America's mountains and rivers,
Such as no bard could achieve in a mean little island like England;
Oft, at the end of a line, the sentence dividing abruptly
Breaks, and in accents mellifluous, follows the thoughts of the author.

ANON.

Tell me not, in idle jingle
  Marriage is an empty dream,
For the girl is dead that's single,
  And things are not what they seem.

Married life is real, earnest,
  Single blessedness a fib,
Taken from man, to man returnest,
  Has been spoken of the rib.

Not enjoyment, and not sorrow,
  Is our destined end or way;
But to act, that each to-morrow
  Nearer brings the wedding-day.

Life is long, and youth is fleeting,
  And our hearts, if there we search,
Still like steady drums are beating
  Anxious marches to the Church.

In the world's broad field of battle,
  In the bivouac of life,
Be not like dumb, driven cattle;
  Be a woman, be a wife!

Trust no Future, how'er pleasant!
  Let the dead Past bury its dead!
Act—act in the living Present.
  Heart within, and Man ahead!

Lives of married folks remind us
  We can live our lives as well,
And, departing, leave behind us;—
  Such examples as will tell;—

Such examples, that another,
  Sailing far from Hymen's port,
A forlorn, unmarried brother,
  Seeing, shall take heart, and court.

Let us then be up and doing,
    With the heart and head begin;
Still achieving, still pursuing,
    Learn to labor, and to win!

PHOEBE CARY

The day is done, and darkness
    From the wing of night is loosed,
As a feather is wafted downward
    From a chicken going to roost.

I see the lights of the baker
    Gleam through the rain and mist,
And a feeling of sadness comes o'er me
    That I cannot well resist.

A feeling of sadness and *longing,*
    That is not like being sick,
And resembles sorrow only
    As a brickbat resembles a brick.

Come, get for me some supper,—
    A good and regular meal,
That shall soothe this restless feeling,
    And banish the pain I feel.

Not from the pastry baker's,
    Not from the shops for cake,
I wouldn't give a farthing
    For all that they can make.

For, like the soup at dinner,
    Such things would but suggest
Some dishes more substantial,
    And tonight I want the best.

Go to some honest butcher,
    Whose beef is fresh and nice
As any they have in the city,
    And get a liberal slice.

Such things through days of labour,
    And nights devoid of ease,
For sad and desperate feelings
    Are wonderful remedies.

77

They have an astonishing power
   To aid and reinforce,
And come like 'Finally brethren',
   That follows a long discourse.

Then get me a tender sirloin
   From off the bench or hook,
And lend to its sterling goodness
   The science of the cook.

And the night shall be filled with comfort,
   And the cares with which it begun
Shall fold up their blankets like Indians,
   And silently cut and run.

                  PHOEBE CARY

The Smithy at St. Mary Cray, in Kent, which (they say) inspired Mr. Longfellow, that poet, to verse, is about to disappear in the rebuilding of High Street. The chestnut tree was destroyed some time ago. As for the poem, I recited it the other day to a man who thought it was the work of Mr. Drinkwater. Hence, I think, it is only right to celebrate the passing of the smithy by some brief appreciation of the Poet and his Message. The more awful literary reviews will probably follow my example shortly; but I doubt if you will understand a word of it. In any case I doubt if they will tell the real story of the Village Blacksmith; which is all the more reason why we should nip in before them now with some exclusive facts which we owe to the research work of Professor Bodger.

It is well known that Mr. Longfellow was first induced to visit the village by Eliza Cook, the poetess with whom he was very friendly; and no doubt when he passed the forge and saw the honest blacksmith the poet's first thought was "How he perspires!" and his second, "I must make a poem about this." Next day the poet passed in the morning, and observed that the honest fellow had just been making a horseshoe; and at evening Mr. Longfellow returned and found that the task was finished.

"Something attempted, I see," said the poet heartily. "And something done."

"Ay, ay, sir," returned the honest blacksmith, touching his forelock respectfully. "It do earn a night's repose."

Mr. Longfellow, struck by this thought, paced slowly home. In the morning the idea for a new poem was practically roughed out; and he said as much to his hostess at breakfast.

"Nothing indelicate, Wadsworth, I hope?" said Miss Eliza Cook, smoothing her black bombazine gown with a nervous hand.

"Certainly not," said Mr. Longfellow sharply. "Why?"

"You will remember," said Miss Eliza Cook, blushing faintly, "that I had to take exception to one stanza of your 'Wreck of the Hesperus,' in which you dwelt so regrettably on the physical charms of the skipp——"

"No sugar, thank you," said the poet coldly.

"I am also," said the lady, averting her gaze, "thinking of your 'Excelsior!' where—correct me, Wadsworth, if I am wrong—a young female is so far lost to modesty and propriety as to invite a passing stranger of the male sex to lay his hand on her breast." And Miss Eliza Cook, a warm wave of colour rushing over her neck, hid her head behind the tea-urn.

"Allow me," said Mr. Longfellow, coughing, "to recite to you a little of my poem." Whereupon, taking a paper from his pocket, the poet began:

> "Under the spreading chestnut tree
> The village smithy stands——"

reading slowly and enunciating each syllable with greatest care, while Miss Eliza Cook beat time with a teaspoon. She listened with rapt attention, only interrupting to beg him to alter

> "His brow is wet with honest sweat"

to

> "Though it transpires he oft perspires"

which (as she justly observed) was equally euphonius and more genteel. Mr. Longfellow politely agreed, and pretended to alter the line in pencil.

"Otherwise," said Miss Eliza Cook, "it is a poem of great beauty and profound philosophy, and entirely free from anything objectionable or licentious. Its influence on English poetry will, I think, be incalculable."

"Baby," said Mr. Longfellow simply, "you said it."

He stayed in England a few weeks longer, hoping to be asked to become Poet Laureate, and then went home to America.

As for William Bashing—known in the village as Honest William —the blacksmith, he continued in his honest way to set an example to his fellow men. Toiling, rejoicing, sorrowing, onward through life he went; each morning saw one task (and no more) begun, each evening saw its close. He was, however, no longer compelled in church on Sunday mornings to wipe away his tear with a hard, rough hand, for a wealthy sympathiser supplied him with handkerchiefs for that purpose; and although his daughter's habit of singing high and shrill above the rest of the choir lost her many friends in the village, it brought many visitors. As the Vicar observed, in the wonderful scheme of Providence there is no evil without some attendant good.

There came to the village one day, when public interest in Honest William seemed to be slackening, a gentleman with an American accent, who walked briskly to the forge and held a short conversation with its pious occupant.

"What's it worth?" said Honest William at length.

"Loud sobs," replied the American gentleman, "two and a half per, sales above 1,000. Soft sobs, one per, sales above 5,000. Twice a Sunday. Double if you mention the poem. Get that?"

Honest William stretched out a large and sinewy hand.

The American gentleman's contribution was in pamphlet form, and ran:

> You Have Heard the Village Blacksmith Sob.
> *Now Buy the Poem.*
> Say "Henry Wadsworth Longfellow" to Your Bookseller.
> It's Worth It.

I admit that it has not the pep, the zip, the punch, the verve of modern specimens. But you must remember that publicity was practically in its infancy then. It served its purpose, at any rate, and Mr. Bashing was able to retire much sooner than he expected.

D. B. WYNDHAM LEWIS

(When Mark Twain gave his "Whittier Birthday Address" in 1877—one of the notorious errata of his career—before a gathering of New England notables in Boston, he thought it would be a harmless piece of buffoonery which would amuse the venerable poets gathered to honor Whittier. As Clemens's biographer, A. B. Paine tells it, when Mark exploded his burlesque in the midst of all that pomp and dignity, it was no minor literary bombshell, but one of planetary size.

("It was an imaginary presentation of three disreputable frontier tramps who at some time had imposed themselves on a lonely miner as Long-fellow, Emerson, and Holmes, quoting apposite selections from their verses to the accompaniment of cards and drink, and altogether conducting themselves in a most unsavory fashion. . . . But Clemens, dazzled by the rainbow splendor of his conception, saw in it only a rare colossal humor, which would fairly lift and bear his hearers along on a tide of mirth. He did not show his effort to any one beforehand. He wanted its full beauty to burst upon the entire company as a surprise.

("After the first two or three hundred words, when the general plan and purpose of the burlesque had developed, when the names of Long-fellow, Emerson, and Holmes began to be flung about by those bleary outcasts, and their verses given that sorry association, those *Atlantic* diners became petrified with amazement and horror. Too late, then, the speaker realized his mistake. He could not stop, he must go on to the ghastly end. And somehow he did it, while as Howells described it 'there fell a silence weighing many tons to the square inch, which deepened from moment to moment, and was broken only by the hysterical and blood-curdling laughter of a single guest.' . . .")

Address of Samuel L. Clemens (Mark Twain) from a report of the dinner given by the publishers of the *Atlantic Monthly* in honor of the Seventieth Anniversary of the Birth of John Greenleaf Whittier, at the Hotel Brunswick, Boston, December 17, 1877, as published in the Boston *Evening Transcript,* December 18, 1877.

MR. CHAIRMAN,—This is an occasion peculiarly meet for the digging up of pleasant reminiscences concerning literary folk, therefore I will drop lightly into history myself. Standing here on the shore of the Atlantic, and contemplating certain of its largest literary billows, I am reminded of a thing which happened to me thirteen years ago, when I had just succeeded in stirring up a little Nevadian literary puddle myself, whose spume-flakes were beginning to blow thinly Californiaward. I started an inspection tramp through the southern mines of California. I was callow and conceited, and I resolved to try the virtue of my *nom de guerre*. I very soon had an opportunity. I knocked at a miner's lonely log cabin in the foothills of the Sierras just at nightfall. It was snowing at the time. A jaded, melancholy man of fifty, barefooted, opened the door to me. When he heard my *nom de guerre* he looked more dejected than before. He let me in—pretty reluctantly, I thought—and after the customary bacon and beans, black coffee and hot whisky, I took a pipe. This sorrowful man had not said three words up to this time. Now he spoke up and said, in the voice of one who is secretly suffering, "You're the fourth—I'm going to move." "The fourth what?" said I. "The fourth littery man that has been here in twenty-four hours—I'm going to move." "You don't tell me!" said I; "who were the others?" "Mr. Longfellow, Mr. Emerson, and Mr. Oliver Wendell Holmes—confound the lot!"

You can easily believe I was interested. I supplicated—three hot whiskies did the rest—and finally the melancholy miner began. Said he:

"They came here just at dark yesterday evening, and I let them in, of course. Said they were going to Yosemite. They were a rough lot, but that's nothing; everybody looks rough that travels afoot. Mr. Emerson was a seedy little bit of a chap, red-headed. Mr. Holmes was as fat as a balloon; he weighed as much as three hundred, and had double chins all the way down to his stomach. Mr. Longfellow was built like a prize-fighter. His head was cropped and bristly, like as if he had a wig made of hairbrushes. His nose lay straight down in his face, like a finger with the end joint tilted up. They had been drinking, I could see that. And what queer talk they used! Mr. Holmes inspected this cabin, then he took me by the buttonhole and says he:

"'Through the deep caves of thought
I hear a voice that sings,

> "Build thee more stately mansions,
> O my soul!' "

"Says I, 'I can't afford it, Mr. Holmes, and moreover I don't want to.' Blamed if I like it pretty well, either, coming from a stranger that way. However, I started to get out my bacon and beans when Mr. Emerson came and looked on awhile, and then *he* takes me aside by the buttonhole and says:

> " 'Give me agates for my meat;
> Give me cantharids to eat;
> From air and ocean bring me foods,
> From all zones and altitudes.'

"Says I, 'Mr. Emerson, if you'll excuse me, this ain't no hotel.' You see, it sort of riled me—I warn't used to the ways of littery swells. But I went on a-sweating over my work, and next comes Mr. Longfellow and buttonholes me and interrupts me. Says he:

> " 'Honor be to Mudjekeewis!
> You shall hear how Pau-Puk-Keewis—'

"But I broke in, and says I, 'Beg your pardon, Mr. Longfellow, if you'll be so kind as to hold your yawp for about five minutes and let me get this grub ready, you'll do me proud.' Well, sir, after they'd filled up I set out the jug. Mr. Holmes looks at it and then he fires up all of a sudden and yells:

> " 'Flash out a stream of blood-red wine!
> For I would drink to other days.'

"By George, I was getting kind of worked up. I don't deny it, I was getting kind of worked up. I turns to Mr. Holmes and says I, 'Looky here, my fat friend, I'm a-running this shanty, and if the court knows herself you'll take whisky straight or you'll go dry.' Them's the very words I said to him. Now I don't want to sass such famous littery people, but you see they kind of forced me. There ain't nothing onreasonable 'bout me. I don't mind a passel of guests a-treadin' on my tail three or four times, but when it comes to *standing* on it it's different, 'and if the court knows herself,' I says, 'you'll take whisky straight or you'll go dry.' Well, between drinks they'd swell around the cabin and strike attitudes

84

and spout; and pretty soon they got out a greasy old deck and went to playing euchre at ten cents a corner—on trust. I began to notice some pretty suspicious things. Mr. Emerson dealt, looked at his hand, shook his head, says—

"I am the doubter and the doubt—'

and calmly bunched the hands and went to shuffling for a new lay-out. Says he:

" 'They reckon ill who leave me out;
They know not well the subtle ways I keep.
I pass and deal *again*!'

Hang'd if he didn't go ahead and do it, too! Oh, he was a cool one! Well, in about a minute things were running pretty tight, but all of a sudden I see by Mr. Emerson's eye he judged he had 'em. He had already corralled two tricks and each of the others one. So now he kind of lifts a little in his chair and says,

" 'I tire of globes and aces!—
Too long the game is played!'

and down he fetched a right bower. Mr. Longfellow smiles as sweet as pie and says,

" 'Thanks, thanks to thee, my worthy friend,
For the lesson thou hast taught.'

and blamed if he didn't down with *another* right bower! Emerson claps his hand on his bowie, Longfellow claps his on his revolver, and I went under a bunk. There was going to be trouble; but that monstrous Holmes rose up, wobbling his double chins, and says he, 'Order, gentlemen; the first man that draws I'll lay down on him and smother him!' All quiet on the Potomac, you bet!

"They were pretty how-come-you-so by now, and they began to blow. Emerson says, 'The noblest thing I ever wrote was "Barbara Frietchie." ' Says Longfellow, 'It don't begin with my "Biglow Papers." ' Says Holmes, 'My "Thanatopsis" lays over 'em both.' They mighty near ended in a fight. Then they wished they had some more company, and Mr. Emerson pointed to me and says:

" 'Is yonder squalid peasant all
That this proud nursery could breed?'

He was a-whetting his bowie on his boot—so I let it pass. Well, sir, next they took it into their heads that they would like some music; so they made me stand up and sing, 'When Johnny Comes March-ing Home' till I dropped—at thirteen minutes past four this morn-ing. That's what I've been through, my friend. When I woke at seven they were leaving, thank goodness, and Mr. Longfellow had my only boots on and his'n under his arm. Says I, 'Hold on there, Evan-geline, what are you going to do with *them?*' He says, 'Going to make tracks with 'em, because—

> " 'Lives of great men all remind us
> We can make our lives sublime;
> And, departing, leave behind us
> Footprints on the sands of time.'

As I said, Mr. Twain, you are the fourth in twenty-four hours—and I'm going to move; I ain't suited to a littery atmosphere."

I said to the miner, "Why, my dear sir, *these* were not the gracious singers to whom we and the world pay loving reverence and homage; these were imposters."

The miner investigated me with a calm eye for a while; then said he, "Ah! imposters, were they? Are you?"

I did not pursue the subject, and since then I have not traveled on my *nom de guerre* enough to hurt. Such was the reminiscence I was moved to contribute, Mr. Chairman. In my enthusiasm I may have exaggerated the details a little, but you will easily for-give me that fault, since I believe it is the first time I have ever deflected from perpendicular fact on an occasion like this.

(Being the only genuine sequel to "Maud Muller")

Maud Muller all that summer day
Raked the meadows sweet with hay;

Yet, looking down the distant lane,
She hoped the judge would come again.

But when he came, with smile and bow,
Maud only blushed, and stammered, 'Ha-ow?'

And spoke of her 'pa,' and wondered whether
He'd give consent they should wed together.

Old Muller burst in tears, and then
Begged that the judge would lend him 'ten';

For trade was dull, and wages low,
And the 'craps' this year were somewhat slow.

And ere the languid summer died,
Sweet Maud became the judge's bride.

But on the day that they were mated,
Maud's brother Bob was intoxicated;

And Maud's relations, twelve in all,
Were very drunk at the judge's hall.

And when the summer came again,
The young bride bore him babies twain.

And the judge was blest, but thought it strange
That bearing children made such a change:

For Maud grew broad and red and stout:
And the waist that his arm once clasped about

Was more than he now could span; and he
Sighed, as he pondered, ruefully,

How that which in Maud was native grace
In Mrs. Jenkins was out of place:

And thought of the twins and wished that they
Looked less like the man that raked the hay

On Muller's farm, and dreamed with pain
Of the day he wandered down the lane,

And, looking down that dreary track,
He half regretted that he came back.

For, had he waited, he might have wed
Some maiden fair and thoroughbred;

For there be women fair as she,
Whose verbs and nouns do more agree.

Alas for maiden! alas for judge!
And the sentimental,—that's one-half 'fudge';

For Maud soon thought the judge a bore,
With all his learning and all his lore

And the judge would have bartered Maud's fair face
For more refinement and social grace.

If, of all words of tongue and pen,
The saddest are, 'It might have been,'

Sadder are these, we daily see,
'It is, but hadn't ought to be.'

BRET HARTE

CHAPTER FOUR

Transcendental Mystics and Bluestocking Reformers

The New Babylon (1840): "Madmen, madwomen, men with beards, Dunkers, Muggletonians, Come-outers, Groaners, Agrarians, Seventh-day Baptists, Quakers, Abolitionists, Calvinists, Unitarians and Philosophers,—all seized their moment to chide, or pray, or preach, or protest."

EMERSON

The Oversoul: A Definition
". . . the spiritual cognescence of psychological ir-refragibility connected with concutient ademption of incoluminent spirituality and etherialized contention of susultory concretion."

ELIZA COOK'S *Journal*

A little reading of the *Dial* will carry you a great way. Eschew, in this case, big words; get them as small as possible, and write them upside down. . . . Put in something about the Supernal Oneness. Don't say a syllable about the Infernal Twoness. Above all, study innuendo. Hint everything—assert nothing. If you feel inclined to say "bread and butter," do not by any means say it outright. You may say everything *approaching* to "bread and butter." You may hint at buckwheat cake, or you may even go so far as to insinuate oat-meal porridge, but if bread and butter be your real meaning, be cautious, my dear Miss Psyche . . .

EDGAR ALLAN POE

In May of the year 1927 I bought a World's Classics edition of "Walden" for, I think, ninety cents and slipped it in my pocket for convenient reading. Since then I have carried it about with me on the cars and in buses and boats, as it is the most amusing detective story I possess. There is, however, a danger in rereading a book, or rather in dipping frequently into the same book: the trouble is you begin to learn some of the lines. In my case, with "Walden," I have recently found that when someone asks me a simple question I reply with a direct quote.

I go into a restaurant, we'll say, at the lunch hour, and the headwaiter approaches me, accusingly.

"All alone?" he asks.

"I feel it wholesome to be alone the greater part of the time," I reply. "To be in company, even with the best, is soon wearisome and dissipating. I love to be alone." Then I glare triumphantly at the waiter and snatch the napkin from the plate.

Or I am walking along the street and meet an acquaintance—someone I haven't seen in a long time and don't care if I never see again.

"Where y'been all this time?" he demands.

"If a man does not keep pace with his companions," I retort, "perhaps it is because he hears a different drummer."

Actually, I suppose, I don't say that at all; yet it often seems to me as though I were saying it. More and more I find it difficult to distinguish clearly between what I am saying and what I might easily be saying. Maybe it's the times. At any rate, Thoreau answers a surprisingly large number of the commonest questions that get thrown at me these days. He is a Johnny-on-the-spot for all ordinary occasions and situations.

I enter a room.

"Won't you sit down?" asks my hostess, indicating a vacancy.

"I would rather sit on a pumpkin and have it all to myself," I reply, accepting the velvet cushion with weary resignation.

"What would you like to drink?" she continues.

"Let me have a draught of undiluted morning air," I snarl. "If men will not drink of this at the fountainhead of the day, why, then, we must even bottle up some and sell it in the shops, for the benefit of those who have lost their subscription ticket to morning time in the world." Then I slump into my cushion and wait for the clear amber liquor and the residual olive.

"Know any good books?" my partner asks at dinner. Slowly I swing my head around, bruising my chin on the hard rough wing of my collar, my eyes glazed with the strain of evening. I place my lips to her ear.

"Much is published," I whisper, cryptically, "but little printed. We are in danger of forgetting the language which all things and events speak without metaphor, which alone is copious and standard."

Or I am at home, getting ready, perhaps, to escort my wife to a soirée.

"What's it like out tonight?" she asks, glancing anxiously at her rubbers in the corner of the closet.

"This is a delicious evening," I hear my voice saying, "when the whole body is one sense, and imbibes delight through every pore."

Next morning, seeing my suit lying rumpled and mussed on the chair beside the bed, she will inquire, "You got anything to go to the presser's?"

"No, my dear," I reply. "Every day our garments become more assimilated to ourselves, receiving the impress of the wearer's character. If you have any enterprise before you, try it in your old clothes." (I am glad to say my wife doesn't mind Thoreau any more and simply calls the presser.)

The situations are endless, the answers inexhaustible. I recall that one of my angriest and boldest retorts was made on a day when a couple of silly giggling girls arrived at our house and began effervescing.

"Isn't this an attractive place?" they squealed.

"On the contrary," I snapped, "I sometimes dream of a larger

93

and more populous house, standing in a golden age, of enduring materials, and without gingerbread work, which shall consist of only one room, a vast rude substantial primitive hall, without ceiling or plastering, with bare rafter and purlins supporting a sort of lower heaven over one's head—useful to keep off rain and snow; where the king and queen posts stand out to receive your homage, when you have done reverence to the prostrate Saturn of an older dynasty on stepping over the sill; a cavernous house, wherein you must reach up a torch upon a pole to see the roof . . . a house whose inside is as open and manifest as a bird's nest."

The girls sobered up instantly, and were quiet and tractable the rest of their visit. But I don't know—I'm afraid I shall have to put "Walden" away and buy another book to travel with. Or possibly a link puzzle. One doesn't remember anything much from long association with a link puzzle.

E. B. WHITE

(The "Boz" dinner in Boston in 1842 which brought forth a group of epistolary parodies by Samuel Kettell—see the selections under *Leatherstocking in Motley*—likewise produced the following burlesque of the transcendental style.)

Sundial Avenue, Feb. 1, 1842

Gentlemen of the Committee—

The wonder-sign of Great Goslington's furibundity is world-absorbing. Quozdom yawns abysmal. Lionized humanity, ephemeral, though, floats upon the time-stream of newspapers and peradventure may avoid fuliginous obliviscity. Scaturient are editor-paragraphs: committee letters no less. Ancient Nicholas shall have his due; why not Liondom? and if Liondom then Quozdom. Penny-trumpetism is orbed:—small-talkism is cubed:—in the abyss of Quozdom ingulfed are both—renascent nevertheless. A dinner is, and it is not.

Savory, committee-gentlemen, is the odor of fried smelts, pork-fat in potatoism pan-borne, harmoniously liquidating. But wherefore fried? Are not gridirons extant in perennial parallelism? Is there lack of culinary capacity in copper stew-pans? Skillets—stand they no longer on three legs in *rerum natura?* Chimneys, methinks, are still redolent of smoke. Nay—Penobscot herrings, even, are world-pickled. Humanity, fish-wise inclined, esurient withal, but antagonizing chowder, might yearn stomach-borne, towards salt mackeral, though ensconced in Barreldom and branded Cargo No. 3.

Truly a world-wonder! But jubilating Quozdom cries, "get out of that!" Patience! O Quozdom—coals are black as ever; and will not water run down hill—Taunton to the contrary notwithstanding? Surely Tag, Rag, and Bobtail are but a dualism: for it is only the Me and the Not-Me, that exist even in Committees and Corporations, pluripersonal although. A pound of butter is the sole type of existence in the life actual, for cheesedom is but a formula. There is no cow, there is no calf; skim-milk alone is. Firkindom is the sappy recipient;—Polly Smallfry the old woman that sells it for ninepence a pound. Avoirdupois is the weight, but don't grease your fingers.

On the time-trodden subject of old shoes, what metaphysics have been expended!—Erebus-like, nevertheless, it frowns repellent; leaving respectable humanity to go barefoot or "toe the mark" in coriaceous integuments. Since calf-skin was made into knapsacks, cobblers have gone in leather aprons. But to Quozdom what avails this?—Gentlemen I incline not dinner-wise. And why? I have dined already. *Pransi;*—enough.

I remain, gentlemen,

MOONSHINE MILKYWATER

What contemporary, if he was in the fighting period of his life,
. . . will ever forget what was somewhat vaguely called the "Transcendental Movement" of thirty years ago? Apparently set astir by
Carlyle's essays on the "Signs of the Times," and on "History," the
final and more immediate impulse seemed to be given by "Sartor
Resartus." At least the republication in Boston of that wonderful
Abraham a Sancta Clara sermon on Lear's text of the miserable
forked radish gave the signal for a sudden mental and mortal mutiny.
Ecce nunc tempus acceptabile! was shouted on all hands with every
variety of emphasis, and by voices of every conceivable pitch, representing the three sexes of men, women, and Lady Mary Wortley
Montagues. . . . Every possible form of intellectual and physical
dyspepsia brought forth its gospel. Bran had its prophets, and the
presartorial simplicity of Adam its martyrs. . . . Plainness of speech
was carried to a pitch that would have taken away the breath of
George Fox; and even swearing had its evangelists, who answered
a simple inquiry after their health with an elaborate ingenuity of
imprecation. . . . Everybody had a mission (with a capital M) to
attend to every-body else's business. No brain but had its private
maggot. . . . Some had an assurance of instant millenium as soon
as hooks and eyes should be substituted for buttons. Communities
were established where everything was to be common, but common
sense. . . . All stood ready at a moment's notice to reform everything but themselves.

JAMES RUSSELL LOWELL

"THE MYSTERIOUS, AMBIGUOUS MR. MELVILLE"

(A somewhat desperate reviewer of *Pierre* resorted to parody to give vent to his feelings about the metaphysical Mr. Melville, prefacing his effort with the following statement: "We really have nothing to add to the severity of the critical notices which have already appeared in respect to this elegantly printed volume; for in all truth, all the notices which we have seen have been severe enough to satisfy the author, as well as the public, that he has strangely mistaken his own powers and the patience of his friends in presuming to leave his native element, the ocean, and his original business of harpooning whales, for the mysteries and ambiguities of metaphysics, love, and romance. It may be, however, that the heretofore intelligible and popular author has merely assumed his present transcendental metamorphosis, in order that he may have range and scope enough to satirize the ridiculous pretensions of some of our modern literati. Under the supposition that such has been his intention, we submit the following notice of his book, as the very best off-hand effort we could make in imitation of his style.")

Melodiously breathing an inane mysteriousness, into the impalpable airiness of our unsearchable sanctum, this wonderful example of its ineffable author's sublime-winging imagination has been fluttering its snow-like-invested pinions upon our multitudinous table. Mysteriously breathing an inane melody, it has been beautifying the innermost recesses of our visual organs with the luscious purpleness and superb goldness of its exterior adornment. We have listened to its outbreathing of sweet-swarming sounds, and their melodious, mournful, wonderful, and unintelligible melodiousness has "dropped like pendulous, glittering icicles," with soft-ringing silveriness, upon our never-to-be-delighted sufficiently organs of hearing; and, in the insignificant significancies of that deftly-stealing and wonderfully-serpentining melodiousness, we have found an infinite, unbounded, inexpressible mysteriousness of nothingness.

ANON. *Godey's Lady's Book*

Miss Birdseye was a little old lady, with an enormous head . . .
a vast, fair, protuberant, candid, ungarnished brow, surmounting a
pair of weak, kind, tired-looking eyes, and ineffectually balanced
in the rear by a cap which had the air of falling backward, and
which Miss Birdseye suddenly felt for while she talked, with un-
successful irrelevant movements. She had a sad, soft, pale face
which looked as if it had been soaked, blurred, and made vague by
exposure to some slow dissolvent. The long practice of philanthropy
had not given accent to her features; it had rubbed out their transi-
tions, their meanings. The waves of sympathy, of enthusiasm, had
wrought upon them in the same way in which the waves of time
finally modify the surface of old marble busts, gradually washing
away their sharpness, their details. In her large countenance her
dim little smile scarcely showed. It was a mere sketch of a smile, a
kind of instalment, or payment on account; it seemed to say that
she would smile more if she had time. . . .
She belonged to the Short-Skirts League, as a matter of course;
for she belonged to any and every league that had been founded
for almost any purpose whatever. This did not prevent her from
being a confused, entangled, inconsequent, discursive old woman,
whose charity began at home and ended nowhere, whose credulity
kept pace with it, and who knew less about her fellow creatures, if
possible, after fifty years of humanity zeal, than on the day she
had gone into the field to protest against the iniquity of most arrangements. . . . She talked continually, in a voice of which the
spring seemed broken, like that of an overworked bell-wire. . . .
No one had an idea how she lived; whenever money was given her
she gave it away to a negro or a refugee. No woman could be less
invidious, but on the whole she preferred these two classes of the
human race. Since the Civil War much of her occupation was gone;

99

for before that her best hours had been spent in fancying that she was helping some Southern slave to escape. It would have been a nice question whether, in her heart of hearts, for the sake of this excitement, she did not sometimes wish the blacks back in bondage. She had suffered in the same way by the relaxation of many European despotisms, for in former years much of the romance of her life had been in smoothing the pillow of exile for banished conspirators. Her refugees had been very precious to her; for she was always trying to raise money for some cadaverous Pole, to obtain lessons for some shirtless Italian. There was a legend that an Hungarian had once possessed himself of her affections, and had disappeared after robbing her of everything she possessed. This was, however, very apocryphal, for she had never possessed anything, and it was open to grave doubt that she could have entertained a sentiment so personal. She was in love, in those days, only with causes, and she languished only for emancipation.

HENRY JAMES, JR.

The Zenith branch of the League of the Higher Illumination met in the smaller ballroom at the Hotel Thornleigh, a refined apartment with pale green walls and plaster wreaths of roses, refined parquet flooring, and ultra-refined frail gilt chairs. Here were gathered sixty-five women and ten men. Most of the men slouched in their chairs and wriggled, while their wives sat rigidly at attention, but two of them—red-necked, meaty men—were as respectably devout as their wives. They were newly rich contractors who, having bought houses, motors, hand-painted pictures, and gentlemanliness, were now buying a refined ready-made philosophy. It had been a toss-up with them whether to buy New Thought, Christian Science, or a good standard high-church model of Episcopalianism.

In the flesh, Mrs. Opal Emerson Mudge fell somewhat short of a prophetic aspect. She was pony-built and plump, with the face of a haughty Pekingese, a button of a nose, and arms so short that, despite her most indignant endeavors, she could not clasp her hands in front of her as she sat on the platform waiting. Her frock of taffeta and green velvet, with three strings of glass beads, and large folding eye-glasses dangling from a black ribbon, was a triumph of refinement.

Mrs. Mudge was introduced by the president of the League of the Higher Illumination, an oldish young woman with a yearning voice, white spats, and a mustache. She said that Mrs. Mudge would now make it plain to the simplest intellect how the Sun Spirit could be cultivated, and they who had been thinking about cultivating one would do well to treasure Mrs. Mudge's words, because even Zenith (and everybody knew that Zenith stood in the van of spiritual and New Thought progress) didn't often have the opportunity to sit at the feet of such an inspiring Optimist and Metaphysical Seer as Mrs. Opal Emerson Mudge, who had lived the Life of Wider Usefulness through Concentration, and in the Silence found those Secrets of Mental Control and the Inner Key which were immediately going to transform and bring Peace, Power, and Prosperity to the unhappy nations; and so, friends, would they for this precious gem-studded hour forget the Illusions of the Seeming Real, and in the actualization of the deep-lying Veritas pass, along with Mrs. Opal Emerson Mudge, to the Realm Beautiful.

If Mrs. Mudge was rather pudgier than one would like one's swamis, yogis, seers, and initiates, yet her voice had the real professional note. It was refined and optimistic; it was overpoweringly calm; it flowed on relentlessly, without one comma, till Babbitt was hypnotized. Her favorite word was "always," which she pronounced olllllle-ways. Her principal gesture was a pontifical but thoroughly ladylike blessing with two stubby fingers.

She explained about this matter of Spiritual Saturation:

"There are those—"

Of "those" she made a linked sweetness long drawn out; a far-off delicate call in a twilight minor. It chastely rebuked the restless husbands, yet brought them a message of healing.

"There are those who have seen the rim and outer seeming of the Logos there are those who have glimpsed and in enthusiasm possessed themselves of some segment and portion of the Logos there are those who thus flicked but not penetrated and radio-activated by the Dynamis go always to and fro assertative that they possess and are possessed of the Logos and the Metaphysikos but this word I bring you this concept I enlarge that those that are not utter are not even inceptive and that holiness is in its definitive essence always always always wholeiness and—"

It proved that the Essence of the Sun Spirit was Truth, but its Aura and Effluxion were Cheerfulness:

"Face always the day with the dawn-laugh with the enthusiasm of the initiate who perceives that all works together in the revolutions of the Wheel and who answers the strictures of the Soured Souls of the Destructionists with a Glad Affirmation—"

It went on for about an hour and seven minutes.

At the end Mrs. Mudge spoke with more vigor and punctuation:

"Now let me suggest to all of you the advantages of the Theosophical and Pantheistic Oriental Reading Circle, which I represent. Our object is to unite all the manifestations of the New Era into one cohesive whole—New Thought, Christian Science, Theosophy, Vedanta, Bahaism, and the other sparks from the one New Light. The subscription is but ten dollars a year, and for this mere pittance the members receive not only the monthly magazine, *Pearls of Healing,* but the privilege of sending right to the president, our revered Mother Dobbs, any questions regarding spiritual progress, matrimonial problems, health and well-being questions, financial difficulties, and—"

SINCLAIR LEWIS

At Concord the Philosophers
    The Whichness of the What . . .
    Have very nearly got
Down to the very essence of

None of them who worship and
    Dub Emerson a saint,
Can clarify the clouds about
    The Notness of the Aint.

J. K. BANGS

CHAPTER FIVE

The Decline and Fall of the House of Usher

"An enthusiasm for Poe is the mark of a decidedly primitive stage of reflection."

HENRY JAMES

"There comes Poe, with his raven, like Barnaby Rudge,
Three-fifths of him genius and two-fifths sheer fudge."

LOWELL

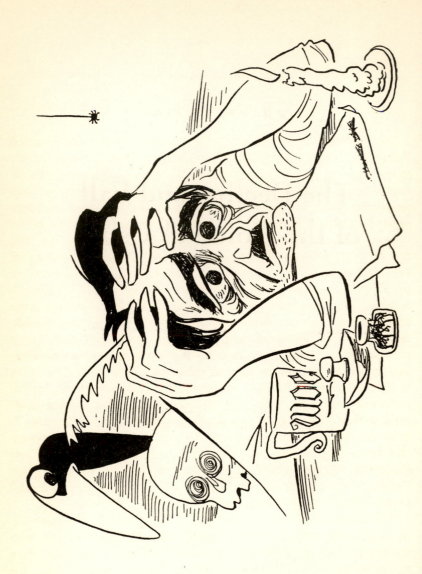

Eulalie, Ulalume, Raven and Bells, Conqueror Worm and Haunted Palace. . . . Was Edgar Allan Poe a major poet? It would surely never occur to any English-speaking critic to say so. And yet, in France, from 1850 till the present time, the best poets of each generation—yes, and the best critics, too; for, like most excellent poets, Baudelaire, Mallarmé, Paul Valéry are also admirable critics —have gone out of their way to praise him. Only a year or two ago M. Valéry repeated the now traditional French encomium of Poe, and added at the same time a protest against the faintness of our English praise. We who are speakers of English and not English scholars, who were born into the language and from childhood have been pickled in its literature—we can only say, with all due respect, that Baudelaire, Mallarmé, and Valéry are wrong and that Poe is not one of our major poets. A taint of vugarity spoils, for the English reader, all but two or three of his poems—the marvelous "City in the Sea" and "To Helen," for example, whose beauty and crystal perfection make us realize, as we read them, what a very great artist perished on most of the occasions when Poe wrote verse. It is to this perished artist that the French poets pay their tribute. Not being English they are incapable of appreciating those finer shades of vulgarity that ruin Poe for us, just as we, not being French, are incapable of appreciating those finer shades of lyrical beauty which are, for them, the making of La Fontaine.

The substance of Poe is refined; it is his form that is vulgar. He is, as it were, one of Nature's Gentlemen, unhappily cursed with incorrigible bad taste. To the most sensitive and high-souled man in the world we should find it hard to forgive, shall we say, the wearing of a diamond ring on every finger. Poe does the equivalent of this in his poetry; we notice the solecism and shudder. Foreign observers do not notice it; they detect only the native gentlemanliness in the poetical intention, not the vulgarity in the details of execution. To them, we seem perversely and quite incomprehensibly unjust.

It is when Poe tries to make it too poetical that his poetry takes on its peculiar tinge of badness. Protesting too much that he is a gentleman, and opulent into the bargain, he falls into vulgarity. Diamond rings on every finger proclaim the parvenu.

Consider, for example, the first two stanzas of "Ulalume."

> The skies they were ashen and sober;
>   The leaves they were crisped and sere—
>   The leaves they were withering and sere;
> It was night in the lonesome October
>   Of my most immemorial year;
> It was hard by the dim lake of Auber,
>   In the misty mid region of Weir—
> It was down by the dank tarn of Auber
>   In the ghoul-haunted woodland of Weir.
>
> Here once, through an alley Titanic
>   Of cypress, I roamed with my soul,
>   Of cypress, with Psyche my soul.
> These were days when my heart was volcanic
>   As the scoriac rivers that roll—
>   As the lavas that restlessly roll
> Their sulphurous currents down Yaanek
>   In the ultimate clime of the pole—
> That groan as they roll down Mount Yaanek
>   In the realms of the boreal pole.

These lines protest too much (and with what a variety of voices!) that they are poetical, and, protesting, are therefore vulgar. To start with, the walloping dactyllic meter is all too musical. Poetry ought to be musical, but musical with tact, subtly and variously. Meters whose rhythms, as in this case, are strong, insistent, and practicably invariable offer the poet a kind of short cut to musicality. They provide him (my subject calls for a mixture of metaphors) with a ready-made, reach-me-down music. He does not have to create a music appropriately modulated to his meaning; all he has to do is to shovel the meaning into the moving stream of the meter and allow the current to carry it along on waves that, like those of the best hairdressers, are guaranteed permanent. Many nineteenth century poets used these metrical short cuts to music, with artistically fatal results.

*   *   *

A quotation and a parody will illustrate the difference between ready-made music and music made to measure. I remember (I trust correctly) a simile of Milton's:

> Like that fair field
> Of Enna, where Proserpine gathering flowers,
>   Herself a fairer flower, by gloomy Dis
> Was gathered, which cost Ceres all that pain
> To seek her through the world.

Rearranged according to their musical phrasing, these lines would have to be written thus:

> Like that fair field of Enna,
>   where Proserpine gathering flowers,
> Herself a fairer flower,
>   by gloomy Dis was gathered,
> Which cost Ceres all that pain
> To seek her through the world.

The contrast between the lyrical swiftness of the first four phrases with that row of limping spondees which tells of Ceres' pain is thrillingly appropriate. Bespoke, the music fits the sense like a glove.

How would Poe have written on the same theme? I have ventured to invent his opening stanza.

> It was noon in the fair field of Enna,
>   When Proserpina gathering flowers—
>   Herself the most fragrant of flowers,
> Was gathered away to Gehenna
>   By the Prince of Plutonian powers;
> Was borne down the winding of Brenner
>   To the gloom of his amorous bowers—
> Down the tortuous highway of Brenner
>   To the god's agapenonous bowers.

The parody is not too outrageous to be critically beside the point; and anyhow the music is genuine Poe. That permanent wave is unquestionably an *ondulation de chez Edgar*. The much too musical meter is (to change the metaphor once more) like a rich chasuble, so stiff with gold and gems that it stands unsupported, a carapace of jeweled sound, into which the sense, like some snotty little seminarist, irrelevantly creeps and is lost. This music of Poe's—how much less really musical it is than that which, out of his nearly neutral decasyllables, Milton fashioned on purpose to fit the slender beauty of Proserpine, the strength and swiftness of the ravisher, and her mother's heavy, despairing sorrow!

*   *   *

How could a judge so fastidious as Baudelaire listen to Poe's music and remain unaware of its vulgarity? A happy ignorance of English versification preserved him, I fancy, from this realization. His own imitations of medieval hymns prove how far he was from understanding the first principles of versification in a language where the stresses are not, as in French, equal, but essentially and insistently uneven. In his Latin poems Baudelaire makes the ghost of Bernard of Cluny write as though he had learned his art from Racine. The principles of English versification are much the same as those of medieval Latin. If Baudelaire could discover lines composed of equally stressed syllables in Bernard, he must also have discovered them in Poe. Interpreted according to Racinian principles, such verses as

> It was down by the dark tarn of Auber
> In the ghoul-haunted woodland of Weir

must have taken on, for Baudelaire, heaven knows what exotic subtlety of rhythm. We can never hope to guess what that ghoul-haunted woodland means to a Frenchman possessing only a distant and theoretical knowledge of our language.

Returning now to "Ulalume," we find that its too poetical meter has the effect of vulgarizing by contagion what would be otherwise perfectly harmless and refined technical devices. Thus, even the very mild alliterations in the "ghoul-haunted woodland of Weir" seem to protest too much. And yet an iambic verse beginning "Woodland of Weir, ghoul-haunted," would not sound in the least overpoetical. It is only in the dactyllic environment that those two w's strike one as protesting too much.

ALDOUS HUXLEY

"A MELLOW CUP OF TEA, GOLDEN TEA"

Here's a mellow cup of tea, golden tea!
What a world of rapturous thought its fragrance bring to me!
    Oh, from out the silver cells
     How it wells!
     How it smells!
Keeping tune, tune, tune
To the tintinnabulation of the spoon.
And the kettle on the fire
Boils its spout off with desire,
With a desperate desire
And a crystalline endeavour
Now, now to sit, or never,
On the top of the pale-faced moon,
But he always came home to tea, tea, tea, tea, tea,
     Tea to the n--th.

BARRY PAIN

"PILLS"

See the doctors with their pills—
    Silver-coated pills!
What a world of misery their calomel instills!
How they twingle, twingle in the icy-golden night.
    You have taken two that mingle.
    And you wish you'd had a single;
While your cheeks are ashy white. . . .

    Oh, the pills, pills, pills—
      Pills, pills, pills!
So ends my riming and my chiming on the pills.

DAMER CAPE

(The following two poems belong in the category of *unconscious* parody. Thomas Holly Chivers out-Heroded both Poe and Swinburne in riming and verbal excesses. A friend of Poe, he asserted after the latter's death that Poe had stolen "The Raven" and other poetical ideas from him. We leave the reader to guess whether they are bad imitations of Poe, or whether "The Raven" is a skillful adaptation of "Isadore.")

While the world lay round me sleeping,
        I alone for Isadore
Patient Vigils lonely keeping,
Someone said to me while weeping:
        "Why this grief forever more?"
And I answered: "I am weeping
        For my blessed Isadore."

Then the Voice again said: "Never
        Shall thy soul see Isadore!
God from me thy love did sever—
He has damned thy soul forever!
        Wherefore then her loss deplore?"

"Back to Hell, thou ghostly Horror!"
        Thus I cried, dear Isadore!
"Phantom of remorseless Sorrow!
Death might from thee pallor borrow—
        Borrow leanness ever more!
Back to Hell again!—tomorrow
        I will go to Isadore!" . . .

(Of these deathless lines, S. Foster Damon in his *Thomas Holly Chivers, Friend of Poe* writes: "Of course we cannot blame a father prostrated with grief over his dead first-born for lacking a sense of humor. But it was the end of Chiver's literary reputation. This Humpty-Dumpty conceit has bid fair to outlive all his other works. Critics had but to quote his own defense, and his case was laughed out of court. And to this day Chivers has mainly been remembered as a montrous parasite upon the fair name of Poe.")

> As an egg, when broken, never
> Can be mended, but must ever
> Be the same crushed egg forever—
>   So shall this dark heart of mine!
> Which, though broken, is still breaking,
> And shall nevermore cease aching
> For the sleep which has no waking—
>   For the sleep which now is thine!

Schin

Once upon a midnight dreary, eerie, scary,
I was wary, I was weary, full of worry, thinking of my lost Lenore,
Of my cheery, airy, faery, fiery Dearie—(Nothing more).
I was napping, when a tapping on the overlapping coping, woke me
    grapping, yapping, groping . . . toward the rapping. I went
    hopping, leaping . . . hoping that the rapping on the coping
Was my little lost Lenore.
That on opening the shutter to admit the latter critter, in she'd
    flutter from the gutter with her bitter eyes a-glitter;
So I opened wide the door, what was there? The dark weir and the
    drear moor,—or I'm a liar—the dark mire, the drear moor,
    the mere door and nothing more!

Then in stepped a stately raven, shaven like the bard of Avon;
    yes, a rovin' grievin' Raven, seeking haven at my door.
Yes, that shaven, rovin' Raven had been movin' (Get me Stephen)
    for the warm and lovin' haven of my stove an' oven door—
Oven door and nothing more.

Ah, distinctly I remember, every ember that December turned from
    amber to burnt umber;
I was burning limber lumber in my chamber that December, and it
    left an amber ember.
With a silken, sad, uncertain flirtin' of a certain curtain,
That old Raven, cold and callous, perched upon the bust of Pallas,
    Just above my chamber door;
(A lusty, trusty, bust, thrust just
    Above my chamber door.)
Had that callous cuss shown malice? Or sought solace, there on Pallas?
    (You may tell us, Alice Wallace.)
Tell this soul with sorrow laden, hidden in the shade an' broodin',—
If a maiden out of Eden sent this sudden bird invadin'
My poor chamber; and protrudin' half an inch above my door.
Tell this broodin' soul (he's breedin' bats by too much sodden'
    readin'—readin' Snowden's ode to Odin)
Tell this soul by nightmare's ridden, if (no kiddin') on a sudden

He shall clasp a radiant maiden born in Aidenn or in Leyden, or
 indeed in Baden Baden—
Will he grab this buddin' maiden, gaddin' in forbidden Eden,
Whom the angels named Lenore?
Then that bird said: "Never more."

"Prophet," said I, "thing of evil, navel, novel, or boll weevil,
You shall travel, on the level! Scratch the gravel now and travel!
Leave my hovel, I implore."
And that Raven never flitting, never knitting, never tatting, never
 spouting "Nevermore,"
Still is sitting (out this ballad) on the solid bust (and pallid)—
 on the solid, valid, pallid bust above my chamber door:
And my soul is in the shadow, which lies floating on the floor,
Fleeting, floating, yachting, boating on the fluting of the matting,—
 Matting on my chamber floor.

C. L. EDSON

The skies they were ashen and sober,
The streets they were dirty and drear;
It was night in the month of October,
  Of my most immemorial year.
Like the skies I was perfectly sober,
  As I stopped at the mansion of Shear,—
At the Nightingale,—perfectly sober,
  And the willowy woodland, down here.

Here, once in an alley Titanic
  Of Ten-pins, I roamed with my soul,—
  Of Ten-pins,—with Mary, my soul:
They were days when my heart was volcanic,
  And impelled me to frequently roll,
  And make me resistlessly roll,
Till my ten-strikes created a panic
  In the realms of the Boreal pole,
Till my ten-strikes created a panic
  With the monkey atop of his pole.

I repeat, I was perfectly sober,
  But my thoughts they were palsied and sere,—
  My thoughts were decidedly queer;
For I knew not the month was October,
  And I marked not the night of the year,
I forgot that sweet *morceau* of Auber
  That the band oft performèd down here,
And I mixed the sweet music of Auber
  With the Nightingale's music by Shear.

And now as the night was senescent,
  And the star-dials pointed to morn,
  And car-drivers hinted of morn,
At the end of the path a liquescent
  And bibulous lustre was born;
'Twas made by the bar-keeper present,
  Who mixèd a duplicate horn,—

His two hands describing a crescent
    Distinct with a duplicate horn.

And I said: 'This looks perfectly regal,
    For it's warm, and I know I feel dry,—
    I am confident that I feel dry;
We have come past the emeu and eagle,
    And watched the gay monkey on high;
Let us drink to the emeu and eagle,—
    To the swan and the monkey on high,—
    To the eagle and monkey on high;
For this bar-keeper will not inveigle,—
    Bully boy with the vitreous eye;
He surely would never inveigle—
    Sweet youth with the crystalline eye.

But Mary, uplifting her finger,
    Said, 'Sadly this bar I mistrust,—
    I fear that this bar does not trust.
O hasten! O let us not linger!
    O fly,—let us fly—ere we must!'
In terror she cried, letting sink her
    Parasol till it trailed in the dust,—
In agony sobbed, letting sink her
    Parasol till it trailed in the dust,—
    Till it sorrowly trailed in the dust.

Then I pacified Mary and kissed her,
    And tempted her into the room,
    And conquered her scruples and gloom;
And we passed to the end of the vista,
    But were stopped by the warning of doom,—
    By some words that were warning of doom;
And I said, 'What is written, sweet sister,
    At the opposite end of the room?'
She sobbed as she answered, 'All liquors
    Must be paid for ere leaving the room.'

Then my heart it grew ashen and sober,
    As the streets were deserted and drear,—

For my pockets were empty and drear;
And I cried, 'It was surely October,
   On this very night of last year,
   That I journeyed,—I journeyed down here,—
   That I brought a fair maiden down here,
   On this night of all nights in the year.'
   Ah! to me that inscription is clear;
Well I know now, I'm perfectly sober,
   Why no longer they credit me here,—
Well I know now that music of Auber,
   And this Nightingale, kept by one Shear.

BRET HARTE

It was many and many a year ago,
  On an island near the sea,
That a maiden lived whom you mightn't know
  By the name of Cannibalee;
And this maiden she lived with no other thought
  Than a passionate fondness for me.

I was a child, and she was a child—
  Tho' her tastes were adult Feejee—
But she loved with a love that was more than love,
  My yearning Cannibalee;
With a love that could take me roast or fried
  Or raw, as the case might be.

And that is the reason that long ago,
  In that island near the sea,
I had to turn the tables and eat
  My ardent Cannibalee—
Not really because I was fond of her,
  But to check her fondness for me.

But the stars never rise but I think of the size
  Of my hot-potted Cannibalee,
And the moon never stares but it bring me nightmares
  Of my spare-rib Cannibalee;
And all the night-tide she is restless inside,
  Is my still indigestible dinner-belle bride,
In her pallid tomb, which is Me,
  In her solemn sepulcher, Me.

C. F. LUMMIS

It was many milenniums long ago
In a houseboat on the mall
That there lived a maiden whom you might know,
Then again, you might not at all.
Ulabel Lume, her high-born name
And she just six feet tall.

I was a child and she was a child
And childishly childlike we'd romp
But we loved with a lovelier love than love
In this old barge on the swamp.
With a love that made winged seraphs in heaven
Foam at the mouth and stomp.

And this was the reason that long ago
The wind came tossin' and pitchin' . . .
My Ulabel Lume was blown off to her doom
From the poop-deck over the kitchen.

So that her high-born kinsmen came
And fished her up out of the blue
And rowed in a dream seven miles upstream.
(Could have made better time by canoe.)

The angels not nearly so happy in heaven
Went envying me and my bride.
Yes! That was the reason (as all men know
In this kingdom here by the tide)
That the heavenly wretches sent down the storm
That whistled her over the side.

But our love (like I said) was more than the love
Of those who were bigger than we,
Even some who were bigger than *she,*
And neither the angels in heaven above
Nor the swamp eels down under the sea
Can ever dissever my soul from the soul
Of my soul where that poor soul may be.

For the moon never beams without bringing me dreams
Of my beautiful Ulabel Lume.
And the dew never damps without bringing me cramps
In the back, in the fog, in the gloom.
And although it's erroneous
All night pneumonious
I lie down by the side of my sweet and euphonious,
In the gloom of the doom of the tomb
Of whom? My long lost, my Ulabel Lume.

BARBARA ANGELL

> . . . *Tenet insanabile multos*
> *Scribendi cacoethes.*
>
> JUVENAL

I did not see the lad. To that I will take an oath—any oath you please, on the Bible, the Koran, or Tooke's Pantheon. I did not see the lad; yet I knew that he was behind me; that he had followed me for several squares up Broadway. I knew that he wore but one shoe; I knew also that he was black, though I will again swear that I did not see his shadow. "How did I know all this?" impatiently demands my reader. Simply by my analytical faculty— by resolving thought into its constituent elements. This was the *magnum arcanum* of my certain, and at first view, mysterious knowledge of these facts. Thus I knew that it was myself, he was following, because, amid all the hurrying crowd, he had maintained so close a proximity, that I could distinctly hear his labored respiration. I knew that he wore but one shoe, by the different sounds made by the two feet in descending. "But how knew you that he was *black?*" I answer, *Ex pede Herculem*—by the peculiar *slapping* sound made by the *bare* foot upon the pavement. That the foot of the Africo-American is *flat,* is a fact sufficiently authenticated by common observation. The somewhat hyperbolical expression, in the popular ballad goes also to confirm it:
"The *hollow* of her foot makes a *hole* in the ground."
Suddenly I turned upon the lad, and said sternly, "Snowball, what want you with me?" The boy absolutely shrieked with surprise and terror, his ebony complexion changed to a ghastly blue, and his enormous eyes rolled up till not a particle of the iris was visible.
When sufficiently recovered, he placed in my hand a soiled and

crumpled note, on reading which, I ordered him to conduct me immediately to a place therein designated. On, on, deeper and deeper, into the most squalid and heaven-forgotten portions of the city, I was led by my urchin guide. At length we paused before a tumble-down-castle of a building—the *ne plus ultra* of all wretchedness, where, after pointing up a crumbling flight of stairs, my ragged cicerone held out his hand for a sixpence. An old woman was standing in the doorway—a fleshless, toothless, half-sightless hag, with grizzly elf-locks straggling over her shrivelled face, munching a crust of mouldy bread, forcibly taken from a starving dog. She took no notice of me, as I passed her to ascend to the third story of the house. The first two or three stairs gave way beneath my feet, probably not having felt the weight of a well-fed person for some years. Shaking from me the dislodged spiders and scorpions which were running in all directions, I shudderingly but safely reached the top of the stairway. Here a door obstructed my passage. To this I found no handle, but perceiving a long, black cord hanging through an aperture, I concluded it was what is called a "latch-string," and gave it a vigorous pull. What was my horror to feel it gliding from my grasp! It was the tail of an enormous rat! Raising my foot, I levelled the door at once, and ascending a second flight of stairs, found myself in a small and most miserable apartment. On a table before me lay a huge pile of manuscripts, beside a bottle, labelled "Ink," but which had been last used as a candlestick. On a wretched bed in one corner was extended the wasted figure of a man. His emaciation was so extreme that in some places the bones were protruding through the skin! His hair and beard, of great length, were grizzly and matted. His nose was transparent in its thinness, and his eyes were sunken almost into invisibility. On the straw at his feet was perched, what at first I took for a raven, but presently discovered to be a wild-visaged black cat, also fearfully attenuated.

The man was insensible—*in articulo mortis,* in fact—but by a few mesmeric passes, and an intense concentration of will, I was able to revive him for a few moments. He opened his eyes—he knew me—I knew *him!* Ay, this forlorn being was the once distinguished Adolphus Twiggs, the poet and novelist; the most successful delineator of the fashionable and sentimental which our country has ever known! "Yes, my friend," he said, "you see before you the victim of the miserable compensation awarded to native genius, and of the want of a law of International Copyright!" Then he added with touching impressiveness, *"Sum quod eris, fui quod sis."*

"How long have you been in this condition?" I asked.

"It is now two years," he replied, "since the Harpers refused to bring out my greatest work, 'Fashionable Flirtations, and Delicate Distresses,' at which time, disgusted with the *punica fides* of both publishers and public, I exiled myself from my kind, and retired to the dignified repose of this garret."

"But, Twiggs, you had a wife?"

"Yes, but I divorced her, *a mensa et thoro*. She was a good creature enough, but no sentiment, no congeniality, and I would not be bored by her. Yes, 'twas a trial, for *inter nos,* Lucy more than half supported us with her needle; but then, what great genius has ever been able long to endure a wife? Since then, that faithful creature (pointing to the cat) has shared my bed and board, and though she can't bring in money, she keeps the rats at a distance, never interrupts me in my inspired moods, and . . ."

Here a fearful change came o'er the sufferer! The cat, who was rubbing against his face, cried out piteously. Twiggs opened his eyes and murmured, "Oh my poor mews!"—then came the death-rattle—the jaw fell, and the ill-rewarded author was no more!

The bereaved cat gave one unearthly howl, turned and sprang frantically into the street below! This was the more easily done, as there was no pane to obstruct her frenzied passage. I drew to the window, and, sick with horror, gazed downward. She had dashed her brains out against the pavement!

GRACE GREENWOOD

CHAPTER SIX

Grains of Sand in
Leaves of Grass

"Oh, yes, a great genius; undoubtedly a very great genius! Only one cannot help deploring his too extensive acquaintance with foreign languages."

HENRY JAMES

"Walt sends me all his books. But tell Walt I am not satisfied—not satisfied. I expect him to make the songs of a nation—but he seems to be contented to —make the inventories."

R. W. EMERSON

"HOME SWEET HOME WITH VARIATIONS"
(As Walt Whitman might have written all around it.)

I.

You over there, young man with the guide book red-bound, covered
      flexibly with red linen,
Come here, I want to talk with you; I, Walt, the Manhattanese,
      citizen of these States, call you.
Yes, and the courier, too, smirking, smug-mouthed, with oiled hair;
      a garlicky look about him generally; him, too, I take in,
      just as I would a coyote, or a king, or a toadstool, or a ham-
      sandwich, or anything or anybody else in the world.
Where are you going?
You want to see Paris, to eat truffles, to have a good time; in Vienna,
      London, Florence, Monaco, to have a good time; you want
      to see Venice.
Come with me. I will give you a good time; I will give you all the
      Venice you want, and most of the Paris.
I, Walt, I call to you. I am all on deck! Come and loaf with me!
      Let me tote you around by your elbow and show you things.
You listen to my ophicleide!
Home!
Home, I celebrate! I elevate my fog-whistle, inspir'd by the thought
      of home.
Come in!—take a front seat; the jostle of the crowd not minding;
      there is room enough for all of you.
This is my exhibition—it is the greatest show on earth—there is no
      charge for admission.
All you have to pay me is to take in my romanza.

II.

1. The brownstone house; the father coming home worried from
      a bad day's business; the wife meets him in the marble-
      paved vestibule; she throws her arms about him; she presses
      him close to her; she looks him full in the face with affec-
      tionate eyes; the frown from his brow disappearing.
   Darling, she says, *Johnny has fallen down and cut his head; the*
   cook is going away and the boiler leaks.

2. The mechanic's dark little third-story room, seen in a flash from the Elevated Railway train; the sewing machine in a corner; the small cook stove; the whole family eating cabbage around a kerosene lamp; of the clatter and roar and groaning wail of the Elevated Train unconscious; of the smell of the cabbage unconscious.

Me, passant, in the train, of the cabbage not quite so unconscious.

3. The French flat; the small rooms, all right angles, unindividual; the narrow halls; the gaudy cheap decorations everywhere.

The janitor and the cook exchanging compliments up and down the elevator shaft; the refusal to send up more coal, the solid splash of the water upon his head, the language he sends up the shaft, the triumphant laughter of the cook, to her kitchen retiring.

4. The widow's small house in the suburbs of the city; the widow's boy coming home from his first day down town; he is flushed with happiness and pride; he is no longer a schoolboy, he is earning money; he takes on the airs of a man and talks learnedly of business.

5. The room in the third class boarding-house; the mean little hard-coal fire, the slovenly Irish servant-girl making it, the ashes on the hearth, the faded furniture, the private provender hid away in the closet, the dreary backyard out the window; the young girl at the glass, with her mouth full of hair-pins, doing up her hair to go downstairs and flirt with the young fellows in the parlour.

6. The kitchen of the old farm-house; the young convict just returned from prison—it was his first offense, and the judges were lenient to him.

He is taking his first meal out of prison; he has been received back, kiss'd, encourag'd to start again; his lungs, his nostrils expand with the big breaths of free air; with shame, with wonderment, with a trembling joy, his heart, too, expanding.

The old mother busies herself about the table; she has ready for him the dishes he us'd to like; the father sits with his back to them, reading the newspaper, the newspaper shaking and rustling much; the children hang wondering around the prodigal—they have been caution'd: *Do not ask where our Jim has been; only say you are glad to see him.*

The elder daughter is there, pale-fac'd, quiet; her young man went back on her four years ago; his folks would not let him marry a convict's sister. She sits by the window, sewing on the children's clothes, the clothes not only patching up; her hunger for children of her own, invisibly patching up.

The brother looks up; he catches her eye, he, fearful, apologetic; she smiles back at him, not reproachfully smiling, with loving pretence of hope, smiling—it is too much for him; he buries his face in the folds of his mother's black gown.

7. The best room of the house, on the Sabbath only open'd; the smell of horse-hair furniture and mahogany varnish; the ornaments on the what-not in the corner; the wax-fruit, dusty, sunken, sagged-in, consumptive-looking, under a glass globe; the sealing-wax imitation of coral; the cigar boxes with shells plastered over; the perforated card-board motto.

The kitchen; the housewife sprinkling the clothes for the fine ironing to-morrow—it is Third-day night, and the plain things are already iron'd, now in cupboards, in drawers, stowed away.

The wife waiting for the husband—he is at the tavern, jovial, carousing; she, alone in the kitchen sprinkling clothes—the little red wood clock with peaked top, with pendulum wagging behind a pane of gaily painted glass, strikes twelve.

The sound of the husband's voice on the still night air,—he is singing: *We won't go home till morning!*—the wife arising, toward the woodshed hastily going, stealthily entering, the voice all the time coming nearer, inebriate, chantant.

The wood-shed; the club behind the door of the woodshed; the wife annexing the club; the husband approaching, always inebriate, chantant.

The husband passing the door of the wood-shed; the club over his head, now with his head in contact; the sudden cessation of song; the temperance pledge signed the next morning; the benediction of peace over the domestic foyer temporarily resting.

III.

I sing the soothing influences of home.
You young man, thoughtlessly wandering, with courier, with guide-
book wandering.
You hearken to the melody of my steam-calliope.
Yawp!

H. C. BUNNER

I happify myself.

I am considerable of a man. I am some. You also are some. We
are all considerable; all are some.

Put all of you and all of me together, and agitate our particles by
rubbing us up into eternal smash, and we should still be some.

No more than some, but no less.

Particularly some, some particularly; some in general, generally
some; but always some, without mitigation.
Distinctly, some!

O ensemble! O quelque-chose!

Some punkins, perhaps;

But perhaps squash, long-necked squash, crooked-necked squash,
cucumber, beets, parsnips, carrots, turnips, white turnips,
yellow turnips, or any sort of sass; long sass, or short sass.

Or potatoes. Men, Irish potatoes; women, sweet potatoes.

Yes, women!

I expatiate myself in female man.

A reciprocity treaty. Not like a jug's handle.

They look at me, and my eyes start out of my head; they speak to
me, and I yell with delight; they shake hands with me, and
things are mixed; I don't know exactly whether I'm them;
or them's me.

Women watch for me; they do. Yes, sir!

They rush upon me; seven women laying hold of one man; and the
divine efflux that thrilled the cosmos before the nuptials of
the saurians overflows, surrounds, and interpenetrates their
souls, and they cry, Where is Walt, our brother? Why does
he tarry, leaving us forlorn?

O, mes soeurs!

Of Beauty.

Of excellence, of purity, of honesty, of truth.

Of the beauty of flat-nosed, pock-marked, pied Congo niggers.

Of the purity of compost-heaps, the perfume of bone-boiling; of the
fragrance of pig-sties, and the ineffable sweetness of general
corruption.

Of the honesty and general incorruptibility of political bosses, or aldermen, of common-council men, of postmasters and government contractors, of members of the House of Representatives, and of government officers generally, of executors of wills, of trustees of estates, of referees, and of cashiers of banks who are Sunday-School superintendents.

Of the truth of theatrical advertisements, and advertisements generally, of an actor's speech on his benefit night, of your salutation when you say, "I am happy to see you, sir," of Mrs. Lydia Pinkham's public confidences, of the miracles worked by St. Jacob's Oil, and the long-recorded virtues of Scheidam schnapps.

I glorify schnapps; I celebrate gin.

In beer I revel and welter. I shall liquor.

Ein lager!

I swear there is no nectar like lager. I swim in it; I float upon it; it heaves me up to heaven; it bears me beyond the stars; I tread upon the ether; I spread myself abroad; I stand self-poised in illimitable space. I look down; I see you; I am no better than you. You also shall mount with me.

Zwei lager!

Encore.

O, my soul!

O, your soul! which is no better than my soul, and no worse, but just the same.

O soul in general! Loafe! Proceed through space with rent garments.

O shirt out-issuing, pendent! O tattered, fluttering flag of freedom! Not national freedom, nor any of that sort of infernal nonsense; but freedom individual, freedom to do just what you d----- (here Mr. Adams gulped the word) please!

By golly, there is nothing in this world so unutterably magnificent as the inexplicable comprehensibility of inexplicableness!

Of mud.

O eternal circles, O squares, O triangles, O hypotenuses, O centres, circumferences, diameters, radiuses, arcs, sines, co-sines, tan-

gents, parallelograms and parallelopipedons! O pipes that
are not parallel, furnace pipes, sewer pipes, meerschaum
pipes, briar-wood pipes, clay pipes! O matches, O fire, and
coal-scuttle, and shovel, and tongs, and fender, and ashes,
and dust, and dirt! O everything! O nothing!
O myself! O yourself!
O my eye!

These things are not in Webster's Dictionary, Unabridged Pictorial;
Nor yet in Worcester's. Wait and get the best.
These have come up out of the ages:
Out of the ground that you crush with your boot-heel:
Out of the muck that you have shoveled away into the compost:
Out of the offal that the slow, lumbering cart, blood-dabbled and
grease-dropping, bears away from the slaughter-house, a
white-armed boy sitting on top of it, shouting Hi! and lick-
ing the horse on the raw, with the bridle.
That much has been many philosophers; that offal was once gods
and sages.
And I verify that I don't see why a man in gold spectacles and a
white cravat, stuck up in a library, stuck up in a pulpit, stuck
up in a professor's chair, stuck up in a governor's chair, or
in a president's chair, should be of any more account than
a possum or a woodchuck.
Libertad, and the divine average!

I tell you the truth. Salut!
I am not to be bluffed off. No, sir!
I am large, hairy, earthy, smell of the soil, am big in the shoulders,
narrow in the flank, strong in the knees, and of an inquiring
and communicative disposition.
Also instructive in my propensities; given to contemplation; am able
to lift anything that is not too heavy.
Listen to me, and I will do you good.
Loafe with me, and I will do you better.
And if any man gets ahead of me, he will find me after him.
Vale!

RICHARD GRANT WHITE

So again, not to be foundered only, but to create from afar, p'raps
what is already brought.

To you, ye irreverent insane grandmother; you, mother-in-law;
you, second cousin twice removed!

A word, maybe two, or three, or four, or five, or six, or seven, or
1,345,843,241,500,400, or more.

O! longitudinal, lop-sided, heterohomogeneous galactic chain of
sovereign, sweltering states, Maine, New Hampshire, Vermont, Massachusetts, Rhode Island, Connecticut. . . . Oregon.

Hi! Towering capitals, great galumptious, big Injun! Augusta of
the Kennebec, Concord on the Merrimac, Montpelier on the
Onion, Boston on Boston Harbor, Providence on Providence
Bay, and Newport on the Narragansett, Hartford on the
Connecticut, and New Haven on New Haven Bay, Allquiet
on the Potomac, Whitman on Paumanok, Tallahassee in-
land.—(Note,—The poet's MS is here lost in space. Vide
Colton's Intermediate Geography, p. 20. Editor.)

O, by Gosh! Succulent tubercle! Sweetblooded—male and female
bulbulient bulb! polite, poligamous potato! Ow! Murphy,
Early Rose, Mercer, Long Red, Peach Blow, Sweet, Un-
sweet, Yellow, South Carolina, North Carolina, Jersey, Ly-
onnaise, Ruta Baga, Horace Greeley.

Cause about these varieties, you can't most always sometimes occasionally, frequently, rarely at intervals, generally, unpre-
meditatively tell.

Bullee!

Sons of the soil arise! Take your mowers! reapers! McCormick,
Buckeye, Woods, Kirby, Clipper, Little Giant, et al, out!

Let your joyful, daily, indigenous Sunday School songs mingle
blend with the too-whit, too-whoo of the owl, cat-bird, crow,
skeeter!

Long, long, long is this darned thing getting,

Bang, bang, bang, che-bang, che-bang!

Hoop-la!

ANON.

(With apologies to Walt Whitman, Plus a Trial Membership in the Classics Club)

A classic waits for me, it contains all, nothing is lacking,
Yet all were lacking if taste were lacking, or if the endorsement of
      the right man were lacking.
O clublife, and the pleasures of membership,
O volumes for sheer fascination unrivalled.
Into an armchair endlessly rocking,
Walter J. Black my president,
I, freely invited, cordially welcomed to membership,
My arm around John Kieran, Hendrick Willem van Loon, Pearl S.
      Buck,
My taste in books guarded by the spirit of William Lyon Phelps
(From your memories, sad brothers, from the fitful risings and
      callings I heard),
I to the classics devoted, brother of rough mechanics, beauty-parlor
      technicians, spot welders, radio-program directors
(It is not necessary to have a higher education to appreciate these
      books),
I, connoisseur of good reading, friend of connoisseurs of good
      reading everywhere,
I, not obligated to take any specific number of books, free to reject
      any volume, perfectly free to reject Montaigne, Erasmus,
      Milton,
I, in perfect health except for a slight cold, pressed for time, having
      only a few more years to live,
Now celebrate this opportunity.
Come, I will make the club indissoluble,
I will read the most splendid books the sun ever shone upon,
I will start divine magnetic groups,
   With the love of comrades,
      With the lifelong love of distinguished committees.

I strike up for an old Book.
Long the best-read figure in America, my dues paid, sitter in arm-

chairs everywhere, wanderer in populous cities, weeping
    with Hecuba and with the late William Lyon Phelps,
Free to cancel my membership whenever I wish.
Turbulent, fleshy, sensible,
Never tiring of clublife,
Always ready to read another masterpiece provided it has the ap-
    proval of my president, Walter J. Black,
Me imperturbe, standing at ease among writers,
Rais'd by a perfect mother and now belonging to a perfect book
    club,
Bearded, sunburnt, gray-neck'd, astigmatic,
Loving the masters and the masters only
(I am mad for them to be in contact with me),
My arm around Pearl S. Buck, only American woman to receive
    the Nobel Prize for Literature,
I celebrate this opportunity.
And I will not read a book nor the least part of a book but has the
    approval of the Committee,
For all is useless without that which you may guess at many times
    and not hit, that which they hinted at,
All is useless without readability.
By God! I will accept nothing which all cannot have their counter-
    part of on the same terms (89¢ for the Regular Edition or
    $1.39 for the De Luxe Edition, plus a few cents postage).
I will make inseparable readers with their arms around each other's
    necks,
  By the love of classics,
    By the manly love of classics.

E. B. WHITE

CHAPTER SEVEN

A Few New Turns of the Screw

"There isn't any third manner. . . . Poor Harry has simply changed his stenographer and the new one records all his hesitancies and ellipses."

WILLIAM JAMES

"There were three periods of his career—James I, James II, and James the Old Pretender."

PHILIP GUEDELLA

("... disastrous was the effect of letting him know that any of his writings had been parodied. I had always regarded the fact of being parodied as one of the surest evidences of fame, and once, when he was staying with us in New York, I brought him with glee a deliciously droll article on his novels by Frank Moore Colby, the author of *Imaginary Obligations,* 1904. The effect was disastrous. I shall never forget the misery, the mortification, even, which tried to conceal itself behind an air of offended dignity. His ever-bubbling sense of fun failed him completely on such occasions."—EDITH WHARTON, *A Backward Glance*)

Some time ago, when Henry James wrote an essay on women that brought to my cheek the hot, rebellious blush, I said nothing about it, thinking that perhaps, after all, the man's style was his sufficient fig-leaf, and that few would see how shocking he really was. And, indeed, it had been a long time since the public knew what Henry James was up to behind that verbal hedge of his, though half-suspecting that he meant no good, because a style like that seemed just the place for guilty secrets. But those of us who had formed the habit of him early could make him out even then, our eyes having grown so used to the deepening shadows of his later language that they could see in the dark, as you might say. I say this not to brag of it, but merely to show that there were people who partly understood him even in *The Sacred Fount,* and he was clearer in his essays, especially in that wicked one on "George Sand: The New Life," published in an American magazine.

Here he was, as bold as brass, telling women to go ahead and do and dare, and praising the fine old hearty goings-on at the court of Augustus the Strong, and showing how they could be brought back again if women would only try. His impunity was due to the sheer laziness of the expurgators. They would not read him, and they did not believe anybody else could. They justified themselves, perhaps, by recalling passages like these in *The Awkward Age*:

"What did this feeling wonderfully appear unless strangely irrelevant. . . ."

"But she fixed him with her weary penetration . . ."

"He jumped at this as if he couldn't bear it, presenting as he walked across the room a large, foolish, fugitive back, on which her eyes rested as on a proof of her penetration. . . ."

"My poor child, you're of a profundity. . . ."

"He spoke almost uneasily, but she was not too much alarmed to continue lucid."

"You're of a limpidity, dear man!"

"Don't you think that's rather a back seat for one's best?"

" 'A back seat?' she wondered with a purity."

"Your aunt didn't leave me with you to teach you the slang of the day."

" 'The slang?' she spotlessly speculated."

Arguing from this that he was bent more on eluding pursuit than on making converts, they let things pass that in other writers would have been immediately rebuked. He had, in fact, written furiously about the proprieties for several years. "There is only one propriety," he said, "that the painter of life can ask of a subject: Does it or does it not belong to life?" He charged our Anglo-Saxon writers with "a conspiracy of silence," and taunted them with the fact that the women were more improper than the men. "Emancipations are in the air," said he, "but it is to women writers that we owe them." The men were cowards, rarely venturing a single, course expression, but already in England there were pages upon pages of women's work so strong and rich and horrifying and free that a man could hardly read them. Halcyon days, they seemed to him, and woman the harbinger of a powerful Babylonish time when the improprieties should sing together like the morning stars. Not an enthusiastic person generally, he always warmed to this particular theme with generous emotion.

His essay on George Sand discussing what he calls the "new life," cited the heart history of that author as "having given her sex for its new evolution and transformation the real standard and measure of change." . . . A life so amorously profuse was sure to set an encouraging example, he thought. Her heart was like an hotel, occupied, he said, by "many more or less greasy males" in

144

quick succession. He hoped the time would come when other women's hearts would be as miscellaneous. . . .

This was plain enough. Any other man would have been suppressed. In a literature so well policed as ours, the position of Henry James was anomalous. He was the only writer of the day whose unconventional notions did not matter. His dissolute and complicated Muse might say just what she chose. Perhaps this was because it would have been so difficult to expose him. Never did so much "vice" go with such sheltering vagueness. Whatever else may be said of James at this time, he was no tempter, and though the novels of this period deal only with unlawful passions, they make but chilly reading on the whole. It is a land where the vices have no bodies and the passions no blood, where nobody sins because nobody has anything to sin with. Why should we worry when a spook goes wrong? For years James did not create one shadow-casting character. His love affairs, illicit though they be, are so stripped to their motives that they seem no more enticing than a diagram. A wraith proves faithless to her marriage vow, elopes with a bogie in a cloud of words. Six phantoms meet and dine, three male, three female, with two thoughts apiece, and, after elaborate geometry of the heart, adultery follows like a Q.E.D. Shocking it ought to be, but yet it is not. Ghastly, tantalizing, queer, but never near enough human to be either good or bad. To be a sinner, even in the books you need some carnal attributes—lungs, liver, tastes, at least a pair of legs. Even the fiends have palpable tails; wise men have so depicted them. No flesh, no frailty; that may be why our sternest moralists licensed Henry James to write his wickedest. They saw that whatever the moral purport of these books, they might be left wide open in the nursery. . . .

There is no doubt that James's style is often too puffed up with its secrets. Despite its air of immense significance, the dark, unfathomed caves of his ocean contain sometimes only the same sort of gravel you could have picked up on the shore. I have that from deep sea thinkers who have been down him. . . .

If the obscurity of the language were due to the idea itself, and if while he tugs at an obstinate thought you could be sure it was worth the trouble, there would be no fault to find, but to him one thing seems as good as another when he is mousing around in a mind. It is a form of self-indulgence. He is as pleased with the motives that lead nowhere as with anything else. It is his even emphasis that most misleads. He writes a staccato chronicle of things both great and small, like a constitutional history half made up of the measures that never passed. And in one respect he does not play fairly. He makes his characters read each other's minds from clues that he keeps to himself. To invent an irreverent instance, suppose I were a distinguished author with a psychological bent and wished to represent two young people as preternaturally acute. I might place them alone together and make them talk like this:

"If—" she sparkled.

"If!" he asked. He had lurched from the meaning for a moment.

"I might"—she replied abundantly.

His eye had eaten the meaning—"Me!" he gloriously burst.

"Precisely," she thrilled. "How splendidly you *do understand*."

I, the distinguished author, versed in my own psychology—the springs of my own marionettes—I understand it perfectly. For me there are words aplenty. But is it fair to you, the reader?

Nevertheless—and this is the main point about Henry James—by indefinable means and in spite of wearisome prolixity he often succeeds in his darkest books in producing very strange and powerful effects. It is a lucky man who can find a word for them. Things you had supposed incommunicable certainly come your way. These are the times when we are grateful to him for pottering away in his nebulous workshop among the things that are hard to express. Even when he fails we like him for making the attempt. We like him for going his own gait, though he leaves us straggling miles behind. We cannot afford at this time to blame any writer who is a little reckless of the average mind.

FRANK MOORE COLBY

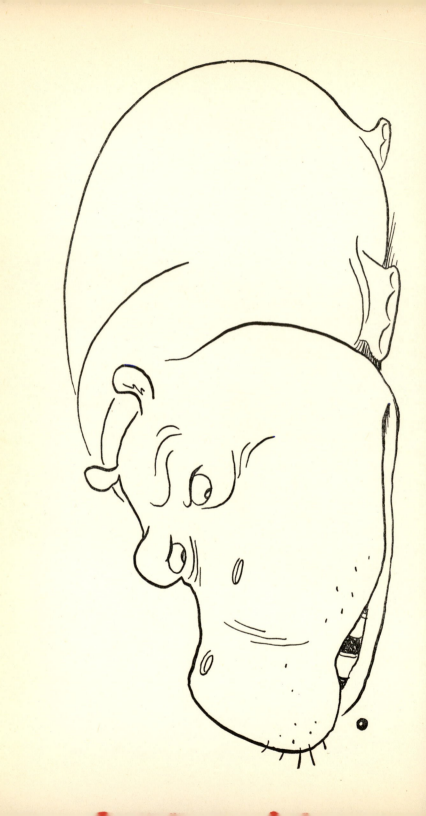

All art too acutely self-centred comes to this sort of thing. James's denatured people are only the equivalent in fiction of those egg-faced, black-haired ladies, who sit and sit, in the Japanese colour prints, the unresisting stuff for an arrangement of blacks. . . .

The only living human motives left in the novels of Henry James are a certain avidity and an entirely superficial curiosity. Even when relations are irregular or when sins are hinted at, you feel that these are merely attitudes taken up, gambits before the game of attainment and over-perception begins. . . . His people nose out suspicions, hint by hint, link by link. Have you ever known living human beings to do that? The thing his novel is *about* is always there. It is like a church lit, but without a congregation to distract you, with every light and line focused on the high altar. And on the altar, very revently placed, intensely there, is a dead kitten, an egg-shell, a bit of string. . . . Like his "Altar of the Dead," with nothing to the dead at all. . . .

Having first made sure that he has scarcely anything left to express, he then sets to work to express it, with an industry, a wealth of intellectual stuff that dwarfs Newton. He spares no resource in the telling of his dead inventions. He brings up every device of language to state and define. Bare verbs he rarely tolerates. He splits his infinitives and fills them up with adverbial stuffing. He presses the passing colloquialism into his service. His vast paragraphs sweat and struggle; they could not sweat and elbow and struggle more if God Himself was the processional meaning to which they sought to come. And all for tales of nothingness. . . . It is leviathan retrieving pebbles. It is a magnificent but painful hippopotamus resolved at any cost, even at the cost of its dignity, upon picking up a pea which has got into a corner of its den. Most things, it insists, are beyond it, but it can, at any rate, modestly, and with an artistic singleness of mind, pick up that pea. . . .

H. G. WELLS

"THE THIRD MANNER"

(Letter of William James to Henry James, May 4, 1907.)

Dearest H.— . . . I've been so overwhelmed with work, and the mountain of the *Unread* has piled up so, that only in these days here have I really been able to settle down to your "American Scene," which in its peculiar way seems to me *supremely great.* You know how opposed your whole "third manner" of execution is to the literary ideals which animate my crude and Orson-like breast, mine being to say a little thing in one sentence as straight and explicit as it can be made, and then to drop it forever; yours being to avoid naming it straight, but by dint of breathing and sighing all round and round it, to arouse in the reader who may have had a similar perception already (Heaven help him if he hasn't!) the illusion of a solid object, made (like the ghost at the Polytechnic) wholly out of impalpable materials, air, and the prismatic interferences of light, ingeniously focused by mirrors upon empty space. . . . But it's the rummest method for one to employ systematically as you do nowadays; and you employ it at your peril. In this crowded and hurried reading age, pages that require such close attention remain unread and neglected. You can't skip a word if you are to get the effect, and 19 out of 20 worthy readers grow intolerant. The method seems perverse: "Say it out, for God's sake," they cry, "and have done with it." And so I say now, give us *one* thing in your older directer manner, just to show that, in spite of your paradoxical success in this unheard of method, you *can* still write according to accepted canons. Give us that interlude; and then continue like the "curiosity of literature" which you have become. For gleams and innuendoes and felicitous verbal insinuations you are unapproachable, but the core of literature is solid. Give it to us *once* again! The bare perfume of things will not support existence, and the effect of solidity you reach is but perfume and similacrum.

150

"A LIMERICK BY HENRY JAMES"

from

The Poets at a House-Party

(A modern mortal having inadvertently stumbled in upon a house-party of poets given on Mount Olympus, being called upon to justify his presence there by writing a poem, offered a Limerick. Whereupon each poet scoffed, and the mortal, offended, challenged them to do better with the same theme.)

THE LIMERICK

A scholarly person named Finck
Went mad in the effort to think
Which were graver misplaced,
To dip pen in his paste,
Or dip his paste-brush in the ink.

(HENRY JAMES' VERSION)

She luminously wavered, and I tentatively inferred that she would soon perfectly reconsider her not altogether unobvious course. Furiously, though with a tender, ebbing similitude, across her mental consciousness stole a re-culmination of all the truths she had ever known concerning, or even remotely relating to, the not-easily fathomed qualities of paste and ink. So she stood, focused in an intensity of soul-quivers, and I, all unrelenting, waited, though of a dim uncertainty whether, after all, it might not be only a dubitant problem.

CAROLYN WELLS

"THE INVOLVULAR CLUB; OR,

THE RETURN OF THE SCREW"

The story had taken hold upon us as we sat round the blazing hearth of Lord Ormont's smoking-room, at Castle Aminta, and sufficiently interfered with our comfort, as indeed from various points of view, not to specify any one of the many, for they were, after all, in spite of their diversity, of equal value judged by any standard, not even excepting the highest, that of Vereker's disturbing narrative of the uncanny visitor to his chambers, which the reader may recall—indeed, must recall if he ever read it, since it was the most remarkable ghost-story of the year—a year in which many ghost-stories of wonderful merit, too, were written—and by which his reputation was made—or rather extended, for there were a certain few of us, including Feverel and Vanderbank and myself, who had for many years known him as a constant—almost too constant, some of us ventured, tentatively, perhaps, but not the less convincedly, to say—producer of work of a very high order of excellence, rivalling in some of its more conspicuous elements, as well as in its minor, to lay no stress upon his subtleties, which were marked, though at times indiscreetly inevident even to the keenly analytical, hinging as these did more often than not upon abstractions born only of a circumscribed environment—circumscribed, of course, in the larger sense which means the narrowing of a circle of appreciation down to the select few constituting its essence—the productions of the greatest masters of fictional style the world has known, or is likely, in view of present tendencies toward miscalled romance, which consists solely of depicting scenes in which bloodshed and murder are rife, soon to know again—it was proper it should, in a company chosen as ours had been from among the members of The Involvular Club, with Adrian Feverel at its head, Vereker as its vice-president, and Lord Ormont, my-self, and a number of ladies, including Diana of the Crossways, and little Maisie—for the child was one of our cares, her estate was so pitiable a one—Rhoda Fleming, Daisy Miller, and the Princess Casamassima, one and all, as the reader must be aware, personages —if I may refer thus to a group of appreciation which included myself—who knew a good thing when they saw it, which, it may as well be confessed at once, we rarely did in the raucous fields of fiction outside of, though possibly at times moderately contiguous to, our own territory, although it should be said that Miss Miller occasionally manifested a lamentable lack of regard for the objects for which The Involvular Club was formed, by showing herself, in her semi-American way, regrettably direct of speech and given over not infrequently to an unhappy use of slang, which we all, save Maisie, who was young, and, in spite of all she knew, not quite so knowledgeable a young person as some superficial ob-servers have chosen to believe, sincerely deprecated, and on occa-sion when it might be done tactfully, endeavored to mitigate by a reproving glance, or by a still deeper plunge into nebulous rhetoric, as a sort of palliation to the Muse of Obscurity, which in our hearts we felt that good goddess would except, strove to offset.

["Excuse me," said Mr. Tom Snobbe, rising and interrupting the reader at this point, "but is all that one sentence, Mr. Jones?"

"Yes," Jones replied. "Why not? It's perfectly clear in its mean-ing. Aren't you used to long sentences on the Hudson?" he added sarcastically.

"No," retorted Snobbe; "that is to say, not where I live. I believe they have 'em at Sing Sing occasionally. But they never get used to them, I'm told."

"Be quiet, Tom," said Harry Snobbe. "It's bad form to inter-rupt. Let Billy finish his story." Mr. Jones then resumed his manu-script.]

A perceptible shudder ran through, or rather rolled over, the group, for it was corrugating in its quality, bringing forcibly to mind, quite as much for its chill, too, as for the wrinkling sugges-tion of its passage up and down our backs, turned as some of these were towards the fire, and others towards the steam radiator, which now and again clicked startlingly in the dull red glow of the hearth light, augmenting the all too obvious nervousness of the listeners, the impassive and uninspiring squares of iron of which certain modern architects of a limited decorative sense—if, indeed, they have any at all, for the mere use of corrugated iron in the construction of a facade would seem not to admit of an aesthetic side to its designer's nature, however ornately distributed over the surface of an exterior it may be—have chosen to avail themselves, prompted either by an appalling parsimony on the part of a client, or for reasons of haste employed for the lack of more immediately available material, it being an undeniable fact that in some portions of the world stucco and terra cotta, now frequently used in lieu of more substantial if not more enduring materials, are difficult of access, and the use of a speedily obtainable substitute becoming thus a requirement as inevitable as it is to be regretted, as in the case of the fruit market at Venice, standing as it does on the bank of the Grand Canal, a pile of stark, staring, obtrusive, wrinkling zinc thrusting itself brazenly into the line of a vision attuned to the most gloriously towering palazzos, as rich in beauty as in romance, with such self-sufficiency as to bring tears to the eyes of the most stolidly unappreciative, of the most coldly unaesthetic, or, in short, as someone has chosen to say, in an essay the title of which and the name of whose author escape us at this moment, with such complacent vulgarity as to amount to nothing less than a dastardly blot upon the escutcheon of the Venetians, which all of their glorious achievements in art, in history, and in letters can never quite ineradically efface, and alongside of which the whistling steam-tugs with their belching funnels, which are by slow degrees supplanting the romantic gondolier with his picturesque costume and his tender songs of sunny climes in the cab service of the Bride of the Adriatic, seem quite excusable, or, in any event, not so unforgivable as to constitute what the Americans would call an infernal shame.

[At this point the reader was interrupted again.

"Hold on a minute, Billy—will you please?" said Tenafly Paterson. "Let's get this story straight. As I understand the first sentence somebody told a ghost story, didn't he?"

"Yes," replied Jones, a trifle annoyed.

"And the second sentence means that those who heard it felt creepy?"

"Precisely."

"Then why the deuce couldn't you have said, 'When So-and-So had finished, the company shuddered'?"

"Because," replied Jones, "I am reading a story which is constructed after the manner of a certain school. I'm not reading a postal card or a cable message."

The reader then resumed.]

Miss Miller, to relieve the strain upon the nerves of those present, which was becoming unbearably tense—and, in fact, poor Maisie had burst into tears with the sheer terror of the climax, and had been taken off to bed by Mrs. Brookenham, who, in spite of many other qualities, was still a womanly woman at heart, and not wholly deficient in those little tendernesses, those trifling but ineffable softnesses of nature, which are at once the chief source of woman's strength and of her weakness, a fact she was constantly manifesting to us during our stay at Lord Ormont's, and which we all remarked and in some cases commented upon, since the discovery had in it some of the qualities of a revelation—began to sing one of those extraordinary popular songs that one hears at the music halls in London, and in the politer and more refined circles of American society, if indeed there may be said to be such a thing in a land so new as to be yet mostly veneer, with little that is solid in its social substructure, beginning as its constituent factors do at the top and working downward, rather than choosing the more natural course of beginning at the bottom and working upward, and which must materially, one may think, affect the social solidarity of the nation by retarding its growth and in otherwise interfering with its healthy, not to say normal development, and which, as the words and import of it come back to me, was known by the rather vulgar and vernacular title of "All Coons Look Alike to Me," thus indicating that the life treated of in the melody, which was not altogether unmusical, and was indeed as a matter of fact quite fetching in its quality, running in one's ears for days and nights long after its first hearing, was that of the negro, and his personal likeness to his other black brethren in the eyes even of one who was supposed to have been at one time, prior to the action of the song if not coincidently with it, the object of his affections.

[Had Jones not been wholly absorbed in the reading of this

wonderful story, he might at this moment have heard a slight but unmistakable rumbling sound, and have looked up and seen much that would have interested him. But, as this kind of a story requires for its complete comprehension a complete comprehension of mind, he did not hear, and so, continuing, did not see.]

Diana was the first to mitigate the silence with comment [he read] a silence whose depth had only been rendered the more depressing by Miss Miller's uncalled-for intrusion upon our mood of something that smacked of a society towards which most of us, in so far as we were able to do so, had always cultivated a strenuous aloofness, prompted not by any whelmful sense of our own perfection, latent or obvious, but rather by a realization on our part that it lacked the essentials that could make of it an interesting part of the lives of a group given over wholly, or at least as nearly wholly as the exiguities of existence would permit of a persistent and continuous devotion, to the contemplation of the beautiful in art, letters, or any other phase of human endeavor.

"And did this soul never thaw? Diana asked.

"Never," replied Vanderbank, "It is frozen yet."

Here the rumbling sound grew to such volume that, absorbed as he was in his reading, Jones could no longer fail to hear it. Lowering his manuscript, he looked sternly upon the company. The rumbling sound was a chorus, not unmusical, of snores.

The Dreamers slept.

"Well, I'll be hanged!" cried Jones angrily, and then he walked over and looked behind the screen where the stenographer was seated. "I'll finish it if it takes all night," he muttered. "Just take this down," he added to the stenographer; but that worthy never stirred or made reply. *He too was sleeping.*

Jones muttered angrily to himself.

"Very well," he said. "I'll read it to myself then," and he began again. For ten minutes he continued, and then on a sudden his voice faltered; his head fell forward upon his chest, his knees collapsed beneath him, and he slid inert, and snoring himself, into his chair. The MS. fluttered to the floor, and an hour later the waiters entering the room found the club unanimously engaged in dreaming once more.

The Involvular Club was too much for them, even for the author of it, but whether this was because of the lateness of the hour or because of the intricacies of the author's style I have never been able to ascertain, for Mr. Jones is very sore on the point, and therefore reticent, and as for the others, I cannot find that any of them remember enough about it to be able to speak intelligently on the subject.

All I do know is what the landlord tells me, and that is that at 5 A.M. thirteen cabs containing thirteen sleeping souls pursued their thirteen devious ways to thirteen different houses, thus indicating that the Dreamers were ultimately adjourned, and, as they have not met since, I presume the adjournment was, as usual, *sine die*.

JOHN KENDRICK BANGS

It was with the sense of a, for him, very memorable something
that he peered now into the immediate future, and tried, not without compunction, to take that period up where he had, prospectively,
left it. But just where the deuce *had* he left it? The consciousness
of dubiety was, for our friend, not, this morning, quite yet clean-
cut enough to outline the figures on what she had called his "horizon," between which and himself the twilight was indeed of a
quality somewhat intimidating. He had run up, in the course of
time, against a good number of "teasers"; and the function of teas-
ing them back—of, as it were, giving them, every now and then,
"what for"—was in him so much a habit that he would have been
at a loss had there been, on the face of it, nothing to lose. Oh, he
always had offered rewards, of course—had ever so liberally pasted
the windows of his soul with staring appeals, minute descriptions,
promises that knew no bounds. But the actual recovery of the article
—the business of drawing and crossing the cheque, blotched though
this were with tears of joy—had blankly appeared to him rather
in the light of a sacrilege, casting, he sometimes felt, a palpable
chill on the fervour of the next quest. It was just this fervour that
was threatened as, raising himself on his elbow, he stared at the
foot of his bed. That his eyes refused to rest there for more than
the fraction of an instant, may be taken—*was,* even then, taken by
Keith Tantalus—as a hint of his recollection that after all the phe-
nomenon wasn't to be singular. Thus the exact repetition, at the
foot of Eva's bed, of the shape pendulous at the foot of *his* was
hardly enough to account for the fixity with which he envisaged it,
and for which he was to find, some years later, a motive in the (as
it turned out) hardly generous fear that Eva had already made the
great investigation "on her own." Her very regular breathing presently reassured him that, if she *had* peeped into "her" stocking, she

must have done so in sleep. Whether he should wake her now, or wait for their nurse to wake them both in due course, was a problem presently solved by a new development. It was plain that his sister was now watching him between her eyelashes. He had half expected that. She really was—he had often told her that she really was—magnificent; and her magnificence was never more obvious than in the pause that elapsed before she all of a sudden remarked "They so very indubitably *are*, you know!"

It occurred to him as befitting Eva's remoteness, which was a part of Eva's magnificence, that her voice emerged somewhat muffled by the bedclothes. She was ever, indeed, the most telephonic of her sex. In talking to Eva you always had, as it were, your lips to the receiver. If you didn't try to meet her fine eyes, it was that you simply couldn't hope to: there were too many dark, too many buzzing and bewildering and all frankly not negotiable leagues in between. Snatches of other voices seemed often to intrude themselves in the parley; and your loyal effort not to overhear these was complicated by your fear of missing what Eva might be twittering. "Oh, you certainly haven't, my dear, the trick of propinquity!" was a thrust she had once parried by saying that, in that case, *he* hadn't—to which his unspoken rejoinder that she had caught her tone from the peevish young women at the Central seemed to him (if not perhaps in the last, certainly in the last but one, analysis) to lack finality. With Eva, he had found, it was always safest to "ring off." It was with a certain sense of his rashness in the matter, therefore, that he now, with an air of feverishly "holding the line," said "Oh, as to that!"

Had *she,* he presently asked himself, "rung off"? It was characteristic of our friend—was indeed "him all over"—that his fear of what she was going to say was as nothing to his fear of what she might be going to leave unsaid. He had, in his converse with her, been never so conscious as now of the intervening leagues; they had never so insistently beaten the drum of his ear; and he caught himself in the act of awfully computing, with a certain statistical passion, the distance between Rome and Boston. He had never been able to decide which of these points he was psychically the nearer to at the moment when Eva, replying "Well, one does, anyhow, leave a margin for the pretext, you know!" made him, for the first time in his life, wonder whether she were not more magnificent than even he had ever given her credit for being. Perhaps it was to test this theory, or perhaps merely to gain time, that he now raised himself to his knees, and, leaning with outstretched arm towards the foot of his bed, made as though to touch the stocking which Santa Claus had, overnight, left dangling there. His posture, as he stared obliquely at Eva, with a sort of beaming defiance, recalled to him something seen in an "illustration." This reminiscence, however—if such it was, save in the scarred, the poor dear old woebegone and so very beguilingly *not* refractive mirror of the moment—took a peculiar twist from Eva's behaviour. She had, with startling suddenness, sat bolt upright, and looked to him as if she were overhearing some tragedy at the other end of the wire, where, in the nature of things, she was unable to arrest it. The gaze she fixed on her extravagant kinsman was of a kind to make him wonder how he contrived to remain, as he beautifully did, rigid. His prop was possibly the reflection that flashed on him that, if *she* abounded in attenuations, well, hang it all, so did *he!* It was simply a difference of plane. Readjust the "values," as painters say, and there you were! He was to feel that he was only too crudely "there" when, leaning further forward, he laid a chubby forefinger on the stocking, causing that receptacle to rock ponderously to and fro. This effect was more expected than the tears which started to Eva's eyes, and the intensity with which "Don't you," she exclaimed, "see?"

"The mote in the middle distance?" he asked. "Did you ever, my dear, know me to see anything else? I tell you it blocks out everything. It's a cathedral, it's a herd of elephants, it's the whole habitable globe. Oh, it's, believe me, of an obsessiveness!" But his sense of the one thing it *didn't* block out from his purview enabled him to launch at Eva's speculation as to just how far Santa Claus had, for the particular occasion, gone. The gauge, for both of them, of this seasonable distance seemed almost blatantly suspended in the silhouettes of the two stockings. Over and above the basis of (presumably) sweetmeats in the toes and heels, certain extrusions stood for a very plenary fulfilment of desire. And, since Eva *had* set her heart on a doll of ample proportions and practicable eyelids—*had* asked that most admirable of her sex, their mother, for

160

it with not less directness than he himself had put into his demand for a sword and helmet—her coyness now struck Keith as lying near to, at indeed a hardly measurable distance from, the borderline of his patience. If she didn't *want* the doll, why the deuce had she made such a point of getting it? He was perhaps on the verge of putting this question to her, when, waving her hand to include both stockings, she said "Of course, my dear, you *do* see. There they are, and you know I know you know we wouldn't, either of us, dip a finger into them." With a vibrancy of tone that seemed to bring her voice quite close to him, "One doesn't," she added, "violate the shrine—pick the pearl from the shell!"

Even had the answering question "Doesn't one just?" which for an instant hovered on the tip of his tongue, been uttered, it could not have obscured for Keith the change which her magnificence had wrought in him. Something, perhaps, of the bigotry of the convert was already discernible in the way that, averting his eyes, he said "One doesn't even peer." As to whether, in the years that have elapsed since he said this either of our friends (now adult) has, in fact, "peered," is a question which, whenever I call at the house, I am tempted to put to one or other of them. But any regret I may feel in my invariable failure to "come up to the scratch" of yielding to this temptation is balanced, for me, by my impression—my sometimes all but throned and anointed certainty—that the answer, if vouchsafed, would be in the negative.

MAX BEERBOHM

CHAPTER EIGHT

Tears and Laughter: The Reading Public

"It depends on a 'happy ending,' on a distribution at
the last of prizes, pensions, husbands, wives, babies,
millions, appended paragraphs, and cheerful remarks."

HENRY JAMES

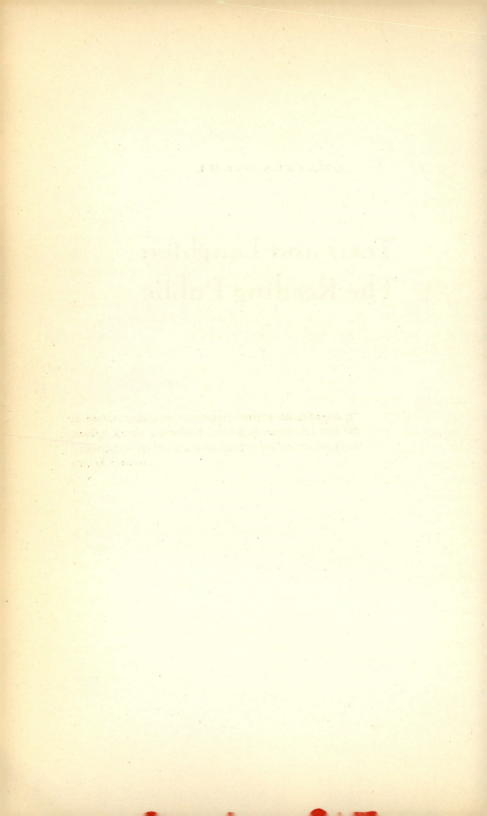

There is a little work in several volumes in our Circulating Library entitled "Little Reading," which I thought referred to a town of that name which I had not been to. There are those who, like cormorants and ostriches, can digest all sorts of this, even after the fullest dinner of meats and vegetables, for they suffer nothing to be wasted. If others are the machines to provide this provender, they are the machines to read it. They read the nine thousandth tale about Zebulon and Sophronia, and how they loved as none had ever loved before, and neither did the course of their true love run smooth,—at any rate how it did run and stumble, and get up again and go on! how some poor unfortunate got up on to a steeple, who had better never have gone up as far as the belfry; and then, having needlessly got him up there, the happy novelist rings the bell for all the world to come together and hear, O dear! how he did get down again! For my part, I think that they had better metamorphose all such aspiring heroes of universal noveldom into man weather-cocks, as they used to put heroes among the constellations, and let them swing round there till they are rusty, and not come down at all to bother honest men with their pranks. The next time the novelist rings the bell I will not stir though the meeting-house burn down. "The Skip of the Tip-Toe-Hop, a Romance of the Middle Ages, by the celebrated author of "Tittle-Tol-Tan," to appear in monthly parts; a great rush; don't all come together." All this they read with saucer eyes, and erect and primitive curiosity, and with unwearied gizzard, . . . just as some little four-year-old bencher his two-cent gilt-covered edition of Cinderella. . . . This sort of gingerbread is baked daily and more sedulously than pure wheat or rye-and-Indian in almost every oven, and finds a surer market.

HENRY DAVID THOREAU

In the evenings of week days he often took her to see plays in which the dazzling heroine was rescued from the palatial home of her treacherous guardian by the hero with the beautiful sentiments. The latter spent most of his time out at soak in pale-green snow-storms, busy with a nickel-plated revolver rescuing aged strangers from villains. Maggie lost herself in sympathy with the wanderers swooning in snow-storms beneath happy-hued church windows, while a choir within sang "Joy to the World." To Maggie and the rest of the audience this was transcendental realism. . . .

In the hero's erratic march from poverty in the first act to wealth and triumph in the final one, in which he forgives all the enemies that he has left, he was assisted by the gallery, which applauded his generous and noble sentiments and confounded the speeches of his opponents by making irrelevant but very sharp remarks. Those actors who were cursed with the parts of villains were confronted at every turn by the gallery. If one of them rendered lines containing the most subtle distinctions between right and wrong, the gallery was immediately aware that the actor meant wickedness, and denounced him accordingly. The last act was a triumph for the hero, poor and of the masses, the representative of the audience, over the villain and the rich man, his pockets stuffed with bonds, his heart packed with tyrannical purposes, imperturbable amid suffering.

STEPHEN CRANE

"HOW LOVE CAME TO GENERAL GRANT"

(In the Manner of Harold Bell Wright)

On a brisk winter evening in the winter of 1864 the palatial Fifth Avenue "palace" of Cornelius van der Griff was brilliantly lighted with many brilliant lights. Outside the imposing front entrance a small group of pedestrians had gathered to gape enviously at the invited guests of the "four hundred" who were beginning to arrive in elegant equipages, expensive ball-dresses and fashionable "swallowtails."

"Hully gee!" exclaimed little Frank, a crippled newsboy who was the only support of an aged mother, as a particularly sumptuous carriage drove up and a stylishly dressed lady of fifty-five or sixty stepped out accompanied by a haughty society girl and an elderly gentleman in clerical dress. It was Mrs. Rhinelander, a social leader, and her daughter Geraldine, together with the Rev. Dr. Gedney, pastor of an exclusive Fifth Avenue church.

"What common looking people," said Mrs. Rhinelander, surveying the crowd aristocratically with her lorgnette.

"Yes, aren't they?" replied the clergyman with a condescending glance which ill befit his clerical garb.

"I'm glad you don't have people like that *dans votre eglise,* Dr. Gedney," said young Geraldine, who thought it was "smart" to display her proficiency in the stylish French tongue. At this moment the door of the van der Griff residence was opened for them by an imposing footman in scarlet livery and they passed into the abode of the "elect."

"Hully gee!" repeated little Frank.

"What's going on to-night?" asked a newcomer.

"Gee—don't youse know?" answered the newsboy. "Dis is de van der Griffs' and to-night dey are giving a swell dinner for General Grant. Dat lady wot just went in was old Mrs. Rhinelander.

I seen her pitcher in de last Harper's Weekly and dere was a story in de paper dis morning dat her daughter Geraldine was going to marry de General."

"That isn't so," broke in another. "It was just a rumor."

"Well, anyway," said Frank, "I wisht de General would hurry up and come—it's getting cold enough to freeze the tail off a brass monkey." The onlookers laughed merrily at his humorous reference to the frigid temperature, although many cast sympathetic looks at his thin threadbare garments and registered a kindly thought for this brave boy who so philosophically accepted the buffets of fate.

"I bet this is him now," cried Frank, and all waited expectantly as a vehicle drove up. The cabman jumped off his box and held the carriage door open.

"Here you are, Miss Flowers," he said, touching his hat respectfully.

A silver peal of rippling laughter sounded from the interior of the carriage.

"Why Jerry," came in velvet tones addressed to the coachman, "You mustn't be so formal just because I have come to New York to live. Call me 'Miss Ella,' of course, just like you did when we lived out in Kansas," and with these words Miss Ella Flowers, for it was she, stepped out of the carriage.

A hush fell on the crowd as they caught sight of her face—a hush of silent tribute to the clear sweet womanhood of that pure countenance. A young man on the edge of the crowd who was on the verge of becoming a drunkard burst into tears and walked rapidly away to join the nearest church. A pr-st---te who had been plying her nefarious trade on the avenue, sank to her knees to pray for strength to go back to her aged parents on the farm. Another young man, catching sight of Ella's pure face, vowed to write home to his old mother and send her the money he had been expending in the city on drinks and dissipation.

And well might these city people be affected by the glimpse of the sweet noble virtue which shone forth so radiantly in this Kansas girl's countenance. Although born in Jersey City, Ella had moved with her parents to the west at an early age and she had grown up in the open country where a man's a man and women lead clean sweet womanly lives. Out in the pure air of God's green places and

170

amid kindly, simple, big-hearted folks, little Ella had blossomed and thrived, the pride of the whole country, and as she had grown to womanhood there was many a masculine heart beat a little faster for her presence and many a manly blush of admiration came into the features of her admirers as she whirled gracefully with them in the innocent pleasure of a simple country dance. But on her eighteenth birthday, her parents had passed on to the Great Beyond and the heartbroken Ella had come East to live with Mrs. Montgomery, her aunt in Jersey City. This lady, being socially prominent in New York's "four hundred," was of course quite ambitious that her pretty little niece from the West should also enter society. For the last three months, therefore, Ella had been fêted at all the better class homes in New York and Jersey City, and as Mrs. van der Griff, the Fifth Avenue social leader, was in the same set as Ella's aunt, it was only natural that when making out her list of guests for the dinner in honor of General Grant she should include the beautiful niece of her friend.

As Ella stepped from the carriage, her gaze fell upon little Frank, the crippled newsboy, and her eyes quickly filled with tears, for social success had not yet caused her to forget that "blessed are the weak." Taking out her purse, she gave Frank a silver dollar and a warm look of sympathy as she passed into the house.

"Gee, there went an angel," whispered the little cripple, and many who heard him silently echoed that thought in their hearts. Nor were they far from wrong.

But even an angel is not free from temptation, and by letting Ella go into society her aunt was exposing the girl to the whisperings of Satan—whisperings of things material rather than things spiritual. Many a girl just as pure as Ella has found her standards gradually lowered and her moral character slowly weakened by the contact with the so-called "refined" and "cultured" infidels one meets in fashionable society. Many a father and mother whose ambition has caused them to have their daughter go out in society have bitterly repented of that step as they watched the poor girl gradually succumbing to the temptation of the world. Let her who thinks it is "smart" to be in society consider that our brothels with their red plush curtains, their hardwood floors and their luxurious appointments, are filled largely with the worn out belles and debutantes of fashionable society.

The next minute a bugle call sounded down the street and up drove a team of prancing grays. Two soldiers sprang down from the coachman's box and stood at rigid attention while the door of the carriage opened and out stepped General Ulysses S. Grant.

A murmur of admiration swept over the crowd at the sight of his manly inspiring features, in which the clean cut virility of a life free from dissipation was accentuated by the neatly trimmed black beard. His erect military bearing—his neat, well-fitting uniform—but above all his frank open face proclaimed him a man's man—a man among men. A cheer burst from the lips of the onlookers and the brave but modest general lowered his eyes and blushed as he acknowledged their greeting.

"Men and women," he said, in a voice which although low, one could see was accustomed to being obeyed, "I thank you for your cheers. It makes my heart rejoice to hear them, for I know you are not cheering me personally but only as one of the many men who are fighting for the cause of liberty and freedom, and for——" the general's voice broke a little, but he mastered his emotion and went on—"for the flag we all love."

At this he pulled from his pocket an American flag and held it up so that all could see. Cheer after cheer rent the air, and tears came to the general's eyes at this mark of devotion to the common cause.

"Wipe the d--d rebels off the face of the earth, G-d, d-- 'em," shouted a too enthusiastic member of the crowd who, I fear, was a little the worse for drink. In an instant General Grant had stepped up to him and fixed upon him those fearless blue eyes.

"My man," said the general, "It hurts me to hear you give vent to those oaths, especially in the presence of ladies. Soldiers do not curse, and I think you would do well to follow their example."

The other lowered his head shamefacedly. "General," he said, "You're right and I apologize."

A smile lit up the general's handsome features and he extended his hand to the other.

"Shake on it," he said simply, and as the crowd roared its approval of this speech the two men "shook."

Meanwhile within the van der Griff house all were agog with excitement in expectation of the arrival of the distinguished guest. Expensively dressed ladies fluttered here and there amid the elegant appointments; servants in stylish livery passed to and fro with trays of wine and other spirituous liquors.

At the sound of the cheering outside, the haughty Mrs. Rhinelander patted her daughter Geraldine nervously, and between mother and daughter passed a glance of understanding, for both felt that to-night, if ever, was Geraldine's opportunity to win the handsome and popular general.

The doorbell rang, and a hush fell over the chattering assemblage; then came the proud announcement from the doorman—"General Ulysses S. Grant"—and all the society belles crowded around the guest of honor.

It had been rumored that the general, being a soldier, was ignorant of social etiquette, but such proved to be far from the case. Indeed, he handled himself with such ease of manner that he captivated all, and for each and every young miss he had an apt phrase or a pretty compliment, greatly to their delight.

"Pleased to know you"—"Glad to shake the hand of such a pretty girl"—"What a nice little hand—I wish I might hold it all evening"—with these and kindred pleasantries the general won the way into the graces of Mrs. van der Griff's fair guests, and many a female heart fluttered in her bosom as she gazed into the clear blue eyes of the soldier, and listened to his well chosen tactful words.

"And how is the dear General this evening?"—this in the affected tone of old Mrs. Rhinelander, as she forced her way through the crowd.

"Finer than silk," replied he, and he added, solicitously, "I hope you have recovered from your lumbago, Mrs. Rhinelander."

"Oh quite," answered she, "And here is Geraldine, General," and the ambitious mother pushed her daughter forward.

"*Comment vous portez vous, mon Général,*" said Geraldine in French. "I hope we can have a nice *tête-a-tête* to-night," and she fawned upon her prey in a manner that would have sickened a less artificial gathering.

Were there not some amid all that fashionable throng in whom ideals of purity and true womanhood lived—some who cared enough for the sacredness of real love to cry upon this hollow mockery that was being used to ensnare the simple, honest soldier? There was only one, and she was at that moment entering the drawing

173

room for the purpose of being presented to the general. Need I name her?

Ella, for it was she, had been upstairs busying herself with her toilet when General Grant had arrived and she now hurried forward to pay her homage to the great soldier. And then, as she caught sight of his face, she stopped suddenly and a deep crimson blush spread over her features. She looked again, and then drew back behind a nearby portiere, her heart beating wildly.

Well did Ella remember where she had seen that countenance before, and as she stood there trembling the whole scene of her folly came back to her. It had happened in Kansas, just before her parents died, on one sunny May morning. She had gone for a walk; her footsteps had led her to the banks of a secluded lake where she often went when she wished to be alone. Many an afternoon had Ella dreamed idly away on this shore, but that day, for some reason, she had felt unusually full of life and not at all like dreaming. Obeying a thoughtless but innocent impulse, with no intention of evil, she had taken off her clothes and plunged thus n-k-d into the cool waters of the lake. After she had swum around a little she began to realize the extent of her folly and she was hurriedly swimming towards the shore when a terrific cramp had seized her lower limbs, rendering them powerless. Her first impulse, to scream for help, was quickly checked with a deep blush, as she realized the consequences if a man should hear her call, for nearby was an encampment of Union soldiers, none of whom she knew. The perplexed and helpless girl was in sore straits and was slowly sinking for the third time, when a bearded stranger in soldier's uniform appeared on the bank and dove into the water. To her horror he swam rapidly towards her—but her shame was soon changed to joy when she realized that he was purposely keeping his eyes tight shut. With a few swift powerful strokes he reached her side, and, blushing deeply, took off his blue coat, fastened it around her, opened his eyes, and swam with her to the shore. Carrying her to where she had left her clothes he stayed only long enough to assure himself that she had completely recovered the use of her limbs, and evidently to spare her further embarrassment, had vanished as quickly and as mysteriously as he had appeared.

Many a night after that had Ella lain awake thinking of the

174

splendid features and the even more splendid conduct of this unknown knight who wore the uniform of the Union army. "How I love him," she would whisper to herself; "but how he must despise me!" she would cry, and her pillow was often wet with tears of shame and mortification at her folly.

It was shortly after this episode that her parents had taken sick and passed away. Ella had come East and had given up hope of ever seeing her rescuer again. You may imagine her feelings then when, on entering the drawing room at the van der Griffs', she discovered that the stranger who had so gallantly and tactfully rescued her from a watery grave was none other than General Ulysses S. Grant.

The poor girl was torn by a tumult of contrary emotions. Suppose he should remember her face. She blushed at the thought. And besides what chance had she to win such a great man's heart in competition with these society girls like Geraldine Rhinelander who had been "abroad" and spoke French.

At that moment one of the liveried servants approached the general with a trayful of filled wine glasses. So engrossed was the soldier hero in talking to Geraldine—or, rather, in listening to her alluring chatter—that he did not at first notice what was being offered him.

"Will you have a drink of champagne wine, General?" said Mrs. van der Griff who stood near.

The general raised his head and frowned as if he did not understand.

"Come, *mon Général,*" cried Geraldine gayly, "We shall drink *à votre succès dans la guerre,*" and the flighty girl raised a glass of wine on high. Several of the guests crowded around and all were about to drink to the general's health.

"Stop," cried General Grant suddenly realizing what was being done, and something in the tone of his voice made everyone pause.

"Madam," said he, turning to Mrs. van der Griff, "Am I to understand that there is liquor in those glasses?"

"Why yes, General," said the hostess smiling uneasily. "It is just a little champagne wine."

"Madam," said the general, "It may be 'just champagne wine' to you, but 'just champagne wine' has ruined many a poor fellow and to me all alcoholic beverages are an abomination. I cannot consent, madam, to remain under your roof if they are to be served. I have never taken a drop—I have tried to stamp it out of the army, and I owe it to my soldiers to decline to be a guest at a house where wine and liquor are served."

An excited buzz of comment arose as the general delivered this ultimatum. A few there were who secretly approved his sentiments, but they were far too few in numbers and constant indulgence in alcohol had weakened their wills so that they dared not stand forth. An angry flush appeared on the face of the hostess, for in society, "good form" is more important than courage and ideals, and by his frank statement General Grant had violently violated the canons of correct social etiquette.

"Very well, Mr. Grant," she said, stressing the "Mr."—"if that's the way you feel about it—"

"Stop," cried an unexpected voice, and to the amazement of all Ella Flowers stepped forward, her teeth clenched, her eyes blazing.

"Stop," she repeated, "He is right—the liquor evil is one of the worst curses of modern civilization, and if General Grant leaves, so do I."

Mrs. van der Griff hesitated for an instant, and then suddenly forced a smile.

"Why Ella dear, of course General Grant is right," she said, for it was well known in financial circles that her husband, Mr. van der Griff, had recently borrowed heavily from Ella's uncle. "There will not be a drop of wine served to-night, and now General, shall we go in to dinner? Will you be so kind as to lead the way with Miss Rhinelander?" The hostess had recovered her composure, and smiling sweetly at the guest of honor, gave orders to the servants to remove the wine glasses.

But General Grant did not hear her; he was looking at Ella Flowers. And as he gazed at the sweet beauty of her countenance he seemed to feel rising within him something which he had never felt before—something which made everything else seem petty and trivial. And as he looked into her eyes and she looked into his, he read her answer—the only answer true womanhood can make to clean, worthy manhood.

"Shall we go *à la salle-à-manger*?" sounded a voice in his ears, and Geraldine's sinuous arm was thrust through his.

General Grant took the proffered talon and gently removed it from him.

"Miss Rhinelander," he said firmly, "I am taking this young lady as my partner," and suiting the action to the word, he graciously extended his arm to Ella who took it with a pretty blush.

It was General Grant's turn to blush when the other guests, with a few exceptions, applauded his choice loudly, and made way enthusiastically as the handsome couple advanced to the brilliantly lighted dining room.

But although the hostess had provided the most costly of viands, I am afraid that the brave general did not fully appreciate them, for in his soul was the joy of a strong man who has found his mate and in his heart was the singing of the eternal song, "I love her—I love her—I love her!"

It was only too apparent to the other guests what had happened and to their credit be it said that they heartily approved his choice, for Mrs. Rhinelander and her scheming daughter Geraldine had made countless enemies with their haughty manners, whereas the sweet simplicity of Ella Flowers had won her numerous friends. And all laughed merrily when General Grant, in his after dinner speech, said "flowers" instead of "flour" when speaking of provisioning the army—a slip which caused both the general and Miss Flowers to blush furiously, greatly to the delight of the good-natured guests. "All the world loves a lover"—truer words were never penned.

After dinner, while the other men, according to the usages of best society, were filling the air of the dining room with the fumes of nicotine, the general, who did not use tobacco, excused himself —amid many sly winks from the other men—and wandered out into the conservatory.

There he found Ella.

"General," she began.

"Miss Flowers," said the strong man simply, "Call me Ulysses."

And there let us leave them.

DONALD OGDEN STEWART

(Aroused by the frank discussion of Birth Control in Mr. Charles G.
Norris's tract, entitled "Seed," as well as by the mention of the same
subject in Mrs. Kathleen Norris's "Passion Flower" and other novels, the
young and impressionable Mr. Riddell attempted in the following to try
his own hand at the all-important theme of limiting our excess productiv-
ity in America. It is of added interest to note that the influence of the
Norris style was so strong that young Riddell, perhaps unconsciously,
framed his treatise in the respective manners of the Norrises themselves.
When this was written, Mrs. Kathleen Norris was already the author
of thirty-three novels.†)

It was early in the summer that Kathy told him that Edgar
Wallace was going to have another novel.

It was a heavenly warm bright shiny clear happy Sunday morning, and the broad green velvety smooth flat rolling croquet field
in the middle of Central Park was filled with gay yellow warm
sunlight. She and Charles were moving idly among the wickets,
swinging their mallets at the smooth fat shiny round balls. Charles
had tried for the stake and missed it, and now he sat on his upended mallet, his smooth fat shiny round face puckered into a frown.

"Edgar thinks he's going to have another novel, Charlie."

"Gosh, that's tough!" Charlie commented absently. He was trying to remember whether he was dead on her.

"He's been typing his eyes out," Kathy continued in a rather
faint voice. "He says the first ten novels aren't so bad, or even
the first twenty," she pursued. "But when you get to write the
fiftieth novel or so, it's terrible."

Charlie extended his toe, slyly moved his ball over an inch or

---

† Thirty-four at the time of going to press.—ed.

two in front of the wicket, and faced her with a great wholesome happy cheerful laugh.

"What's terrible, honey?" he asked.

"The novel, of course!" she conceded honestly. "Charlie," she went on suddenly, deliberately, not looking at him as she knocked her ball into position for the center wicket, "I wonder how you'd feel if I were going to have another novel?"

"I know how I'd feel," Charlie said promptly; "I'd take it out into a vacant lot somewhere and burn it!"

"Oh, Charlie, why?" Kathy asked, widening her big dark round bright eyes reproachfully. "Everybody writes them." Her cheeks were suddenly red, and her eyes full of tears. "Look at Faith Baldwin, or Hugh Walpole, or Mary Roberts Rinehart, or Mazo de la Roche, or Margaret Ayer Barnes—they deliver one every year. Sometimes they even have twins."

"Well, if I was in Edgar's place," Charlie said, as he judged his distance and then rapped the stake smartly, "I'd go to my publishers and have them decide that the public couldn't stand another novel just now, that they'd have to save his reputation by—well, cutting it out."

"Oh, but Charlie! Isn't that a terribly wrong thing to do?"

"What's wrong with it?"

"Well—well—" She stopped, puzzled and a little sick. "It seems so unfair to the novel. It—it ought to have its little chance."

"Don't you think the public ought to have a chance, too?"

"But—but there seems to be something so humiliating about it," Kathy faltered, her cheeks burning. "To have a whole season go by without being on the best-seller lists! To have to give up the first-serial rights—and the second-serial rights—and the movie rights— and the foreign rights—"

"It isn't half as bad, I should think, as writing it," Charlie argued.

"Oh, no, Charlie, that's natural!"

"I don't know about that," Charlie began, laying his mallet down and pointing an argumentative forefinger at the woman before him. "I've been doing a lot of thinking about this whole subject of book-control. Of course, my publishers don't agree with me. They believe that the practice of Literary Contraception profanes the sacrament of Inspiration, and is a frustration of the creative instinct in

Art. It is my opinion, however, that reckless breeding should be checked for the sake of the author's reputation. It unquestionably takes the lives of thousands of writers annually, ruins the careers of as many more, and in addition brings hundreds of thousands of diseased, crippled and deformed novels into the world that should never have been written. Some of them die, many linger on in dire poverty, shivering in their paper jackets, while others roam at large, doubtless interbreeding in the movies and producing a weak and imbecile line of sequels that threatens to lower the whole stock of American literature.

"Several authors that you and I know are—or were—examples of such reckless breeding. You may recall, Kathy, an author by the name of John Erskine?"

"Very well."

"His history came to my attention very forcibly the other day in a Liggett's window. He's confined now in the dollar reprints; but before he was put where he couldn't do any further harm, he had brought a weak and helpless novel into the world named *Unfinished Business,* which was totally unable to exist alone, and was forced to depend on its older sister Helen and its brother Galahad for its entire support. Thus the future happiness of two healthy novels was threatened by this imbecile brother; and the poor author— whose health had been none too good after having *Adam and Eve* and *Uncle Sam*—went into a serious decline."

He shook his head.

"The saddest case is that of Emil Ludwig. After writing the life of everyone else, the poor fellow has now produced a biography of himself!"

"Uncle Emil! Himself?"

"Pitiful case. A fine talent gone to pot-boiling. He had a publisher in New York and he bore him one volume after another. After Emil had delivered six or seven books in rapid succession, however, the public grew tired of him, disappeared at intervals, rejected a couple. You wouldn't know him today; he's beaten in spirit, in substance, in artistic integrity. The biography-racket has crushed him body and soul. You can't deny it, legal book-control undoubtedly would have been a blessing to Uncle Emil."

Kathy leaned weakly on her mallet. The warm bright sunny

cheerful Park swam before her, the croquet-wickets, stakes, balls, and idle spectators seemed blurred before her eyes.

"You look kind of white yourself, Kathy," interrupted Charles curiously.

"I don't know—I'm all right, I guess."

"You've been having too many novels in the last few years," he said solicitously. "Every three months or so. It weakens you, honey. *Passion Flower* was too much for you—let alone *Margaret Yorke*."

The very title made waves of nausea sweep over her. She clutched her mallet and swung listlessly at the croquet-ball before her. It went short of the wicket.

"A lot of other American authors present interesting phases of this same problem," continued Charlie, hitting his ball deftly between two wickets, and rapping the stake. "Take the late James Branch Cabell, for instance. He was undoubtedly one of the outstanding figures of our era; but he did not know the meaning of book-control. Overproduction weakened him, and he died in giving birth to his last novel. If he had practiced literary contraception, he might have been alive today. Let me see—are you still for the middle wicket?"

Kathy shook her head vaguely. She was thinking again of her panic-stricken visit to her publisher this very morning and her face burned, and her hands were dry. A business-like man; it was nothing to him. No, there was no question about Mrs. Norris's condition; she was scheduled for his fall lists. He was sorry, but he did not know any way out of it now. It would be extremely expensive to remove it at this date. He never advised it.

It was like a nightmare. Her publisher had removed her last doubt. This was no longer fear: it was terrible certainty.

"I'm going to have a novel. In October."

No, she did not have the courage to tell Charlie. She dragged herself across the court, and swung dizzily again at the ball. Charlie smiled as it wired itself behind the wicket, and he took his turn, grasping the mallet firmly as he elaborated further on his favorite theme: "There is one thing more I'd like to bring up about this question, and I'm done. It requires approximately three novels a year to sustain our present-day novelists, if they depend on royalties alone. The average number of novels born of literate stock is 2.8; while those of men and women from the pulpwoods is 97.2. You can clearly see where book-control is being practiced. In order to save the decent novelists from bringing about a complete suicide of American literature, not only must they publish more, but the fecundity of the illiterate writers must be curtailed. It must be obvious to anyone who stops to consider the situation at all that our intellectual class of writers is dying out, and the cheaper novelists and less mentally fit are on the increase; it must necessarily follow that our standard of national literature will decline and continue to decline."

He paused and drew out a sheaf of notes from his hip pocket. Kathy saw the scene rapidly growing black before her eyes; she felt herself swaying guiltily as Charlie read the climax of his argument aloud.

"The crux of the whole situation is simply this: our intelligent writers are not producing, and our ignorant, inferior ones are. Unless book-control is stopped among the upper classes, and its use legalized among the lower classes, the best part of our literature will die off, and the country will be over-run by incompetents and morons—"

There was a little moan, and then a faint thud behind him. Kathy had fainted.

"Kathy! Kathy!"

She found herself stretched upon the wooden bench at the side of the croquet field. Her teeth chattered, and Charlie, who was fumbling about vaguely, pale with concern and sympathy, held her hands.

"You're freezing!"

"Don't look so scared, Charlie!"

She laughed frantically, her teeth still chattering. He stared at her sympathetically.

"Anything I could do for you, Kath?" He was not thinking of what he was saying. Her heart beat fast, and she regarded him steadily, not moving a muscle. Suddenly, in an odd tone, he began, "Kathy—"

She looked at him, turning over to lie on her back, her face flushed, her hands icy, and her head rocking.

"Kath," he said, clearing his throat. "Have you thought—you know, this might be—"

Kath swallowed with a dry throat and patted his hand.

"It is, Charlie," she whispered, with a little effort.

182

"How d'you know?" he asked quickly.

"I asked a publisher. Our publisher."

"And he said—?"

"—Said there was no mistake about it. It is due some time in October."

"He—What do you know about that?" Charlie stammered, his face lighted with bewilderment and surprise. "You poor kid," he added awkwardly.

Kathy's cold fingers continued to cling tightly to his hand; she watched him anxiously.

"Isn't there some way to—get out of it, Kath?" Charlie asked presently, a little doubtfully. "You've had thirty-three, you see. I just thought maybe—well, remember, you're not as strong as you were—you see, the last ten or twelve you've had have all died—"

Her pale face grew whiter, and gripping his hand, with sudden fear and entreaty in her voice, she said:

"Charlie, I won't. It means—no, I couldn't do that. Getting rid of your own novel! That's—that's badder, to me, than not writing a novel at all. Think of it, dear—not to have the name of Norris on the best-seller lists this fall—"

"Well, now, I don't know about that," said Charlie in a queer strained voice.

"Charlie!" She looked up at him in sudden comprehension. "You don't mean that you—"

Suddenly she was sitting up, her arm tightly about him, her wet cheek pressed against his. He spoke after a long pause, his eyes lowered guiltily.

"It's true, Kathy. My publisher told me today. I'm going to have a novel in October myself."

She was laughing joyfully, exultantly.

"Then all this that you were saying about literary contraception, and book-control, and our country being over-run by incompetents and morons—you don't mean a word of it?"

"Of course I mean it," he affirmed stoutly. "I'm strongly in favor of book-control—"

She stared at him in bewilderment.

"—for everybody else," he concluded hastily.

The Norrises embraced together in perfect understanding.

COREY FORD

183

After reading an early edition of Ella Wheeler Wilcox's "Poems of Passion," with preface by the author.

Of course they said some horrid things about you,
And lent shocked ears to the sweet songs you sung,
And told each other there could be no doubt you
Were a corrupting influence to the young;
But time has passed, the ultimate revealer;
And as today I read your early song,
I cannot but remark, oh, Ella Wheeler,
They done you wrong.

For the first time I've read your "Pomes of Passion,"
And your proud words of maidenly defense;
I was brought up on modern lyric fashion,
Which knows no prunes or prisms or pretense.
Were you today, with all your youthful ardor,
Sounding the cadences of love's young dream,
You would, I fear, find it a great deal harder
To be "extreme."

Today a girl who wants to be a poet
First learns from Freud what all behavior means,
And then cuts loose, and lets the public know it
By red-hot verses in the magazines.
Then, you apologized for palpitating,
And made excuses for your sapphic fires—
Today you would be calmly celebrating
Suppressed desires.

Yet I suppose you were a bit elated
By all the fuss your lovelorn lyrics made;
You had a public hardly educated
To calling much of anything a spade.
Yes, you were lucky to have been exciting
And to have caused a moralistic row—
You'd not be equal to the sort of writing
That shocks us now!   STODDARD KING

Mr. Jack Oak-hearse calmly rose from the table and shot the bar-tender of Tomato Can, because of the objectionable color of his hair. Then Mr. Oak-hearse scratched a match on the sole of his victim's boot, lit a perfumed cigarette and strolled forth into the street of the camp to enjoy the evening air. Mr. Oak-hearse's face was pale and impassive, and stamped with that indefinable hauteur that marks the professional gambler. Tomato Can knew him to be a cool, desperate man. The famous Colonel Blue-bottle was reported to have made the remark to Miss Honorine-Sainte-Claire, when that leader of society opened the Pink Assembly at Toad-in-the-Hole, on the other side of the Divide, that he, Colonel Blue-bottle, would be everlastingly "----ed if he didn't believe that that ----ed Oak-hearse would open a ----ed jack-pot on a pair of ----ed tens, ----ed ef he didn't." To which Miss Ste.-Claire had responded:

"Fancy now."

On this occasion as Mr. Jack Oak-hearse stepped in the cool evening air of the Sierra's from out of the bar of the hotel of Tomato Can, he drew from his breast pocket a dainty manicure set and began to trim and polish his slender, almost feminine finger nails, that had been contaminated with the touch of the greasy cards. Thus occupied he betook himself leisurely down the one street of Tomato Can, languidly dodging an occasional revolver bullet, and stepping daintily over the few unburied corpses that bore mute testimony to the disputatious and controversial nature of the citizens of Tomato Can. He arrived at his hotel and entered his apartments, gently waving aside the half-breed Mexican who attempted to disembowel him on the threshold. The apartment was crudely furnished as befitted the rough and ready character of the

185

town of Tomato Can. The Wilton carpet on the floor was stained with spilt Moet and Chandon. The full-length portrait of Mr. Oak-hearse by Carolus Duran was punctured with bullet-marks, while the teakwood escritoire, inlaid with buhl and jade, was encumbered with bowie knives, spurs, and Mexican saddles.

Mr. Oak-hearse's valet brought him the London and Vienna papers. They had been ironed and scented with orris-root, and the sporting articles blue-penciled. "Bill," said Mr. Oak-hearse, "Bill, I believe I told you to cut out all the offensive advertisements from my papers; I perceive, with some concern, that you have neglected it. Your punishment shall be that you will not brush my silk hat next Sunday morning."

The valet uttered an inarticulate cry and fell lifeless to the floor.

"It's better to stand pat on two pair than to try for a full hand," mused Mr. Oak-hearse, philosophically, and his long lashes drooped wearily over his cold steel-blue eyes, like velvet sheathing a poignard.

A little later the gambler entered the dining-room of the hotel in evening dress, and wearing his cordon of the Legion of Honor. As he took his accustomed place at the table, he was suddenly aware of a lustrous pair of eyes that looked into his cold gray ones from the other side of the catsup bottle. Like all heroes, Mr. Jack Oak-hearse was not insensible to feminine beauty. He bowed gallantly. The lady flushed. The waiter handed him the menu.

"I will have a caviar sandwich," affirmed the gambler with icy impassivity. The waiter next handed the menu to the lady, who likewise ordered a caviar sandwich.

"There is no more," returned the waiter. "The last one has just been ordered."

Mr. Oak-hearse started, and his pale face became even paler. A preoccupied air came upon him, and the lines of an iron determination settled upon his face. He rose, bowed to the lady, and calmly passed from the dining-room out into the street of the town and took his way toward a wooded gulch hard by.

When the waiter returned with the caviar sandwich he was informed that Mr. Oak-hearse would not dine that night. A triangular note on scented mauve paper was found at the office begging the lady to accept the sandwich from one who had loved not wisely but too many.

But next morning at the head of the gulch on one of the largest pine trees the searchers found an ace of spades (marked) pinned to the bark with a bowie knife. It bore the following, written in pencil with a firm hand:

Here lies the body of
JOHN OAK-HEARSE
who was too much of a gentleman
to play a Royal-flush
against a Queen-full.

And so, pulseless and cold with a Derringer by his side and a bullet in his brain, though still calm as in life lay he who had been at once the pest and the pride of Tomato Can.

FRANK NORRIS

CHAPTER NINE

Vox Pop in the Forum

"Here comes the orator, with his flood of words, and his drop of reason."

POOR RICHARD

"But as they hedn't no gret things to say,
And sed 'em often, I come right away."

JAMES RUSSELL LOWELL

Delivered at Fort Vancouver W. T., on the Fourth of July, 1856, by John Phoenix, S. D., Sergeant Major, Eighty-Third Regiment, Oregon Territory Light Mules.

"BROTHER SOLDIERS AND FELLOW CITIZENS:—
I feel honored by the call that I have received and accepted to deliver on this great occasion, the glorious anniversary of our nation's independence, the customary oration. . . .
"Throughout our whole vast extent of country, from Hancock Barracks, Houlton, Maine, where they pry the sun up in the morning, to Fort Yuma on the Colorado-River, where the thermometer stands at 212° in the shade, and the hens lay hard-boiled eggs, this day will be a day of hilarity, of frolicking and rejoicing.
". . . For on this day the great American eagle flaps her wings, and soars aloft, until it makes your eyes sore to look at her, and looking down upon her myriads of free and enlightened children, with flaming eye, she screams, 'E Pluribus Unum,' which may be freely interpreted, 'Aint I some?' and myriads of freemen answer back with joyous shout: 'You *are* punkins!' . . . And what is the cause of this general rejoicing, this universal hilarity, this amiable state of feeling, this love and veneration for this particular day of all days in the year—a day when the native American forgets all prejudices, and, though loving his country better than aught else, feels well disposed toward every thing besides—a day that our German population respect and speak of as 'more better as good' —a day which Pat, who believes one man is as good as another, and a mighty sight better, reverences as he does 'Saint Patrick's in the morning'—a day when aught unpleasant is forgotten, and mirth, and jollity, and fire-crackers abound. I will endeavor to inform you. Many years ago . . . there dwelt in the far-off city of Genoa, a

191

worthy merchant named Daniel Lumbus, who prosecuted his business as a dealer in velvets, under the name and style of Lumbus & Co.

"This merchant, at a somewhat advanced age, was blest with a son of great promise, whom, out of compliment to his partners, he named Christopher Co Lumbus. . . .

". . . Christopher sailed in 1492, and after the most unheard-of trials and difficulties, encountered many head-winds, and much opposition from his crew, finally . . . discovered this continent, which, from its discoverer, derived the name of America. Then New England was discovered by John Cabot, and Virginia by Walter Raleigh, who also discovered tobacco, and give himself dyspepsia by smoking it to excess, and Pocahontas was discovered by John Smith, and South Carolina by Calhoun.

"Emigration from Great Britain and other countries then commenced, and continued to a tremendous extent, and all our forefathers, and eight grandfathers, came over and settled in the land.

"They planted corn and built houses, they killed the Indians, hung the Quakers and Baptists, burned the witches alive, and were very happy and comfortable indeed. So matters went on very happily, the colonies thus formed owing allegiance to the government of Great Britain until the latter part of the eighteenth century, when a slight change took place in their arrangements. The king of Great Britain, a Dutchman of the name of George Guelph, No. 3, having arrived at that stage of life when Dutchmen generally, if at all inclined that way, naturally begin to give way to ill-temper and obstinacy, became of a sudden exceedingly overbearing and ill-disposed toward the colonies.

". . . By this time it suddenly occured to some of the smartest of our respectable ancestors that it was a good long way to the little island of England, that there was a good many people in the provinces, and that perhaps they were quite as able to govern themselves as George Guelph No. 3 was to govern them. They accordingly appointed delegates from the various Provinces or States, who, meeting together in Philadelphia on the fourth day of July 1776, decided to trouble the King of England no longer, and gave to the world that glorious Declaration of Independence, to the support of which they pledged their lives, their fortunes, and their sacred honor. . . .

"Love of country is strongly impressed on every mind; but, as

Americans, we should and in fact do have this feeling more strongly developed than any other citizens of the world. For our country is a free country; its institutions are wise and liberal, and our advantages as its natives are greater than those of other citizens. To be sure, every body can vote two or three times in some places; it is true taxes are four and a half per cent on the amount of our property; it's a fact that it's difficult to get scrip paid; there's no disputing the existence of the Maine Liquor Law; and we do occasionally have a mob; but these are errors not arising from the principles of our government, but from circumstances, and they will finally obviate and correct themselves. Upon the whole, I believe that a man has quite as much chance for a life of happiness if born under the glorious stars and stripes as if he happened to be born anywhere else, and perhaps a little more. We elect our own rulers, and make our own laws, and if they don't turn out well, it's very easy at the next election to make others in their place. Every body has a chance for distinction in this country; nothing is wanting but natural ability to attain it; and Mrs. Laving Pike's baby, now lying with a cotton-flannel shirt on, in a champagne basket, in Portland, O. T., has just as good a chance of being president of the United States, as the imperial infant of France, now sucking his royal thumbs in his silver cradle at Paris, has of being an emperor. I do not wish to flatter this audience; I do not intend to be thought particularly complimentary; but I do assure you, that there is not a man present who, if he had votes enough, might not be elected president of the United States. And this important fact is the result not so much of any particular merit or virtue on your part, as of the nature of our glorious, liberal, republican institutions.

"In this great and desirable country, any man may become rich, provided he will make money; and man may be well educated, if he will learn, and has money to pay for his board and schooling; and any man may become great, and of weight in the community, if he will take care of his health, and eat sufficiently of boiled salmon and potatoes.

"Moreover, I assert it unblushingly, any man in this country may marry any woman he pleases—the only difficulty being for him to find any woman that he does please. . . .

". . . An anecdote that went the round of the papers a few years since is amusing and interesting, as showing the independent feeling engendered in the minds of all classes by the arrival of the glorious Fourth.

"A parsimonious merchant who, I regret to say, flourished in Boston, kept his counting-room open on Independence Day, where he sat with his clerk, a boy of ten or twelve years of age, busy over his accounts, while the noise and uproar of the celebration were resounding without. Looking up from his employment, he perceived the unfortunate youth, perched upon his high stool, engaged in picking his nose, a practice that the merchant had frequently reprobated, and taken him to task for.

" 'William,' he exclaimed, 'why will you persist in that dirty practice? I am astonished at you.'

" 'I don't care,' whimpered the unhappy boy. 'It's Independence day, and it's my own nose, and I'll pick thunder out of it.'

". . . I have never known a Fourth of July oration delivered, and I have listened to many, without a full and complete biography of the immortal Washington being given before its conclusion. It may appear a slightly hackneyed custom, but I shall certainly not let you go off without it. At the risk of appearing tedious, I shall therefore request your patience for a few moments, while I read from the 'Clatrap Cyclopedia,' by Professor Tube Rose, the following beautiful tribute to the memory of this greatest of men:

[From Tube Rose's American Biography.]
" 'GENERAL GEORGE WASHINGTON.

"George Washington was one of the most distinguished movers in the American Revolution.

"He was born of poor but honest parents, at Genoa, in the year 1492. His mother was called the mother of Washington. He married, early in life, a widow lady, Mrs. Martha Custis, whom Prescott describes as the *cussidest* pretty woman south of Mason and Dixon's line.

". . . Although, for the time in which he lived, a very distinguished man, the ignorance of Washington is something perfectly incredible. He never travelled on a steam-boat; never saw a railroad, or a locomotive engine; was perfectly ignorant of the principle of the magic of the magnetic telegraph; never had a daguerreotype, Colt's pistol, Sharp's rifle, or used a friction match. He ate his meals with an iron fork, never used postage-stamps on his letters, and knew

194

nothing of the application of chloroform to alleviate suffering, or the use of gas for illumination. Such a man as this could hardly be elected president of the United States in these times, although, it must be confessed, we occasionally have a candidate who proves not much better informed about matters in general.

"Washington died from exposure on the summit of Mount Vernon, in the year 1786, leaving behind him a name that will endure forever, if posterity persist in calling their children after him to the same extent that has been fashionable. He is mentioned in history as having been 'first in peace, first in war, and first in the hearts of his countrymen'; in other words, he was No. 1 in everything, and it was equally his interest and his pleasure to look out for that number, and he took precious good care to do so. A portrait, by Gilbert Stuart, of this great soldier and statesman may be seen, very badly engraved, on the 'History of the United States'; but as it was taken when the general was in the act of chewing tobacco, the left cheek is distended out of proportion, and the likeness rendered very unsatisfactory. . . .

"Accustomed as I am to public speaking, it has been with no ordinary distrust of my own powers that I have ventured to address you to-day. Standing beneath the waving banner of our country, with Mount Hood towering in snow-crowned magnificence above our heads, and the broad bosom of the noble Columbia spread in calm expanse at our feet, I see before me an attentive audience composed of individuals whose interest I am proud to awaken and command. I see before me some who have borne no undistinguished part in the bloody but most righteous war now raging in our vicinity; I see men who have pushed the war into the enemy's country with the gallant Haller, and returned with him when he thought, perhaps, it would be about as well to leave; who accompanied the daring and skillful Raines, when intrepidly rushing with drawn sword at the head of his troops into Father Pandosy's hut, he wrote that letter to the humbled Kamiakin; men who have planned and built block-houses, which serve alike as refuges from the attacks of the savage and merciless foe, and imperishable monuments of architectural taste and refinement. These services which have brought this war so nearly to a close, (for already the Sun of peace may be seen gilding the clouds in the east preparatory to rising,) are well worthy of commendation; and no better occasion can be found to recapitulate and commemorate them than the present.

". . . In future times, when by some impartial historian the present Oregon war is faithfully depicted, posterity, as it peruses the volume, will drop a tear o'er the picture of the sufferings of those noble volunteers that wallowed in the Walla Walla valley, and their intrepid march into that country, and their return, will excite a thrill of admiration as an adventure never equaled even by Napoleon H. Bonaparte, when he effected the passage of the Alps.

But the war will soon be ended; it is even now drawing to a close. The completion of the Pacific railroad, which may be looked upon as certain in the course of the next fifty years, increasing our facilities for transportation of arms and supplies, will undoubtedly have a most favorable effect; and I look upon it as a matter of little doubt that, three or four hundred years from this time, hostilities will have ceased entirely, and the Indians will have been liberally treated with, and become quiet and valuable members of our society.

The influence of that glorious banner will have been felt by them; they will have been made to see stars; they will have been compelled to feel stripes; and all will be peace and harmony, love and joy among them. Four hundred years from this time, the decendants of Kamiakin will be celebrating with our posterity the recurrences of this glorious day, with feelings of interest and delight. While to-day that great chief, moved by feelings of animosity toward us, sits and gnaws the gambrel-joint of a defunct Cayuga pony, little knowing on which side of his staff of life the oleaginous product of lactation is disseminated. But long after that time shall arrive, centuries and centuries after our difficulties shall have been settled, and the scrip, with accumulated interest, paid, may our glorious institutions continue to flourish, may the Union be perpetuated forever in perfect bonds of strength and fraternal affection, and the

> "Star-spangled banner continue to wave
> O'er the land of the free and the home of the brave."

Music by the Band

JOHN PHOENIX

When the Senator arrived the church was crowded, the windows were full, the aisles were packed, so was the vestibule, and so, indeed, was the yard in front of the building. As he worked his way through to the pulpit on the arm of the minister and followed by the envied officials of the village, every neck was stretched and every eye twisted around intervening obstructions to get a glimpse. Elderly people directed each other's attention and said, "There! that's him, with the grand, noble, forehead!"

The Senator took his seat in the pulpit, with the minister on one side of him and the superintendent of the Sunday-school on the other. The town dignitaries sat in an impressive row within the altar railings below. The Sunday-school children occupied ten of the front benches, dressed in their best and most uncomfortable clothes, and with hair combed and faces too clean to feel natural. So awed were they by the presence of a living United States Senator, that during three minutes not a "spit-ball" was thrown. . . .

Senator Dilworthy arose and beamed upon the assemblage for a full minute in silence. Then he smiled with an excess of sweetness upon the children and began:

"My little friends—for I hope that all these bright-faced little people are my friends and will let me be their friend—my little friends, I have travelled much, I have been in many cities and many states, everywhere in our great and noble country, and by the blessing of Providence I have been permitted to see many gatherings like this—but I am proud, I am truly proud to say that I never have looked upon so much intelligence, so much grace, such sweetness of disposition as I see in the charming young countenances I see before me at this moment. I have been asking myself, as I sat here, Where am I? Am I in some far-off monarchy, looking upon little princes and princesses? No. Am I in some populous center of my own country, where the choicest children of the land have been selected and brought together as at a fair for a prize? No. Am I in some strange foreign clime where the children are marvels that we know not of? No. Then where am I? Yes—where am I? I am in a simple, remote, unpretending settlement of my own dear state, and these are the children of the noble and virtuous men who have made me what I am! My soul is lost in wonder at the thought! And I humbly thank Him to whom we are but as worms in the dust, that He has been pleased to call me to serve such men! Earth has no higher, no grander position for me. Let kings and emperors keep their tinsel crowns, I want them not; my heart is here!

"Again I thought, Is this a theater? No. Is it a concert or a gilded opera? No. Is it some other vain, brilliant, beautiful temple of soul-staining amusement and hilarity? No. Then what is it? What did my consciousness reply? I ask you, my little friends, What did my consciousness reply? It replied, It is the temple of the Lord! Ah, think of that, now. I could hardly keep the tears back, I was so grateful. Oh, how beautiful it is to see these ranks of sunny little faces assembled here to learn the way of life; to learn to be good; to learn to be useful; to learn to be pious; to learn to be great and glorious men and women; to learn to be props and pillars of the State and shining lights in the councils and the households of the nation; to be bearers of the banner and soldiers of the cross in the rude campaigns of life, and ransomed souls in the happy fields of Paradise hereafter.

"Children, honor your parents and be grateful to them for providing for you the precious privileges of a Sunday-school.

"Now, my dear little friends, sit up straight and pretty—there, that's it—and give me your attention and let me tell you about a poor little Sunday-school scholar I once knew. He lived in the Far West, and his parents were poor. They could not give him a costly education, but they were good and wise and they sent him to the Sunday-school. He loved the Sunday-school. I hope you love your Sunday-school—ah, I see by your faces that you do! That is right.

"Well, this poor little boy was always in his place when the bell rang, and he always knew his lesson; for his teachers wanted him to learn and he loved his teachers dearly. Always love your teachers, my children, for they love you more than you can know now. He would not let bad boys persuade him to go to play on Sunday.

There was one little bad boy who was always trying to persuade him, but he never could.

"So this poor little boy grew up to be a man, and had to go out in the world, far from home and friends, to earn his living. Temptations lay all about him, and sometimes he was about to yield, but he would think of some precious lesson he learned in his Sunday-school a long time ago, and that would save him. By and by he was elected to the legislature. Then he did everything he could for Sunday schools. He got laws passed for them; he got Sunday schools established wherever he could.

"And by and by the people made him governor—and he said it was all owing to the Sunday-school.

"After a while the people elected him a representative to the Congress of the United States, and he grew very famous. Now temptations assailed him on every hand. People tried to get him to drink wine, to dance, to go to theaters; they even tried to buy his vote; but no, the memory of his Sunday-school saved him from all harm; he remembered the fate of the bad little boy who used to try to get him to play on Sunday, and who grew up and became a drunkard and was hanged. He remembered that, and was glad he never yielded and played on Sunday.

"Well, at last what do you think happened? Why the people gave him a towering, illustrious position, a grand, imposing position. And what do you think it was? What should you say it was, children? It was Senator of the United States! That poor little boy that loved his Sunday-school became that man. *That man stands before you!* All that he is, he owes to the Sunday-school.

"My precious children, love your parents, love your teachers, love your Sunday-school, be pious, be obedient, be honest, be diligent, and then you will succeed in life and be honored of all men. Above all things, my children, be honest. Above all things be pure-minded as the snow. Let us join in prayer."

MARK TWAIN

"THE TREASURER'S REPORT"

Author's Note

About eight years ago (eight, to be exact) I was made a member of a committee to plan a little Sunday night entertainment for some newspapermen who wanted to act. The committee was supposed to meet at a certain time, each member with some suggestions for sketches or song-numbers. (In order to get out of this morass of pussy-footing which I have got myself into, I will come right out and say that the "certain time" at which the committee was to meet was 8 P.M. on Sunday night.) At 7:15 P.M. I suddenly realized that I had no suggestions to offer for the entertainment.

As all the other members of the committee were conscientious workers, I felt considerably abashed. But as they were also charming and indulgent fellows, I knew that they would take my dereliction in good part if I could only take their minds off the business of the meeting and possibly put them in good humor with a comical story or a card-trick. So, on my way up in the taxi, I decided to make believe, when they called on me for my contribution, that I had misunderstood the purpose of the committee-meeting and had come prepared to account for the year's expenditures. These I jotted down on the back of an old shirt.

As is always the case with such elaborate trickery, my plan to escape censure by diverting the minds of the committee fell flat. They listened to my temporizing report and voted me a droll chap, but then they said: "And now what are your suggestions for the entertainment?" As I had to confess that I had none, it was agreed that, *faute de mieux,* I should elaborate the report I had just offered and perhaps acquire some skill in its delivery, and give that as my share of the Sunday night entertainment. At this moment my entire life changed its course.

200

I guess that no one ever got so sick of a thing as I, and all my friends, have grown of this Treasurer's Report. I did it every night and two matinees a week for nine months in the Third Music Box Revue. Following that, I did it for ten weeks in vaudeville around the country, I did it at banquets and teas, at friend's houses and in my own house, and finally went to Hollywood and made a talking movie of it. In fact, I have inflicted it on the public in every conceivable way except over the radio and dropping it from airplanes. But I have never written it. I have been able to throw myself into a sort of trance while delivering it, so that the horrible monotony of the thing made no impression on my nerve cells, but to sit down and put the threadbare words on paper has always seemed just a little too much to bear.

I am writing it out now more as a release than anything else. Perhaps, in accordance with Freudian theories, if I rid myself of this thing which has been skulking in the back of my mind for eight years, I shall be a normal man again. No one has to read it. I hope that no one does, for it doesn't read at all well. All I want to do is get it on paper and out of the way. I feel better already, just from having told all this. And please let's never bring the matter up again.

The report is delivered by an Assistant Treasurer who has been called in to pinch-hit for the regular Treasurer who is ill. He is not a very good public-speaker, this assistant, but after a few minutes of confusion is caught up by the spell of his own oratory and is hard to stop.

I shall take but a very few moments of your time this evening, for I realize that you would much rather be listening to this interesting entertainment than to a dry financial statement . . . but I *am* reminded of a story—which you have probably all of you heard.

It seems that there were these two Irishmen walking down the street when they came to a—oh, I should have said in the first place that the parrot which was hanging out in *front* of the store— or rather belonging to one of these two fellows—the *first* Irishman, that is—was—well, anyway, this parrot—

(*After a slight cogitation, he realizes that, for all practical purposes, the story is as good as lost; so he abandons it entirely and, stepping forward, drops his facile, story-telling manner and assumes a quite spurious businesslike air.*)

Now, in connection with reading this report, there are one or two points which Dr. Murnie wanted brought up in connection with it, and he has asked me to bring them up in connec—to bring them up.

In the first place, there is the question of the work which we are trying to do up there at our little place at Silver Lake, a work which we feel not only fills a very definite need in the community but also fills a very definite need—er—in the community. I don't think that many members of the Society realize just how big the work is that we are trying to do up there. For instance, I don't think that it is generally known that most of our boys are between the age of fourteen. We feel that, by taking the boy at this age, we can get closer to his real nature—for a boy *has* a very real nature, you may be sure—and bring him into closer touch not only with the school, the parents, and with each other, but also with the town in which they live, the country to whose flag they pay allegiance, and to the—ah—(*trailing off*) town in which they live.

Now the fourth point which Dr. Murnie wanted brought up was that in connection with the installation of the new furnace last Fall. There seems to have been considerable talk going around about this not having been done quite as economically as it might—have—been—done, when, as a matter of fact, the whole thing *was* done just as economically as possible—in fact, even *more* so. I have here a report of the Furnace Committee, showing just how the whole thing was handled from start to finish.

(*Reads from report, with considerable initial difficulty with the stiff covers.*)

Bids were submitted by the following firms of furnace contractors, with a clause stating that if we did not engage a firm to do the work for us we should pay them nothing for submitting the bids. This clause alone saved us a great deal of money.

The following firms, then, submitted bids:

Merkle, Wybigant Co., the Eureka Dust Bin and Shaker Co., The Elite Furnace Shop, and Harris, Birnbauer and Harris. The bid of Merkle, Wybigant being the lowest, Harris Birnbauer **was** selected to do the job.

(*Here a page is evidently missing from the report, and a hurried search is carried on through all the pages, without result.*)

Well, that pretty well clears up that end of the work. Those of you who contributed so generously last year to the floating hospital have probably wondered what became of the money. I was speaking on this subject only last week at our up-town branch, and, after the meeting, a dear little old lady, dressed all in lavender, came up on the platform, and, laying her hand on my arm, said: "Mr. So-and-So (calling me by name) Mr. So-and-So, what the hell did you do with all the money we gave you last year?" Well, I just laughed and pushed her off the platform, but it has occurred to the committee that perhaps some of you, like that little old lady, would be interested in knowing the disposition of the funds.

Now, Mr. Rossiter, unfortunately our treasurer—or rather Mr. Rossiter our *treasurer, unfortunately* is confined at his home to-night with a bad head-cold and I have been asked (*he hears someone whispering at him from the wings, but decides to ignore it*) and I have been asked if I would (*the whisperer will not be denied, so he goes over to the entrance and receives a brief message, returning beaming and laughing to himself*). Well, the joke seems to be on *me!* Mr. Rossiter has *pneumonia!*

Following, then, is a summary of the Treasurer's Report:

(*Reads, in a very businesslike manner.*)

During the year 1929—and by that is meant 1928—the **Choral** Society received the following in donations:

B. L. G.	$500
G. K. M.	500
Lottie and Nellie W.——	500
In memory of a happy summer at Rye Beach	10
Proceeds of a sale of coats and hats left in the boat-house	14.55
And then the Junior League gave a performance of "Pinafore" for the benefit of the Fund, which, unfortunately, resulted in a deficit of	300

Then, from dues and charges	2,354.75
And, following the installation of the new furnace, a saving in coal amounting to $374.75—which made Dr. Murnie very happy, you may be sure.	
Making a total of receipts amounting to	3,645.75

This is all, of course, reckoned as of June.

In the matter of expenditures, the Club has not been so fortunate. There was the unsettled condition of business, and the late Spring, to contend with, resulting in the following—er—rather discouraging figures, I am afraid:

Expenditures	$23,574.85
Then there was a loss, owing to—several things—of	3,326.70
Car-fare	4,452.25
And then, Mrs. Rawlins' expense account, when she went down to see the work they are doing in Baltimore, came to $256.50, but I am sure that you will all agree that it was worth it to find out—er—what they are doing in Baltimore.	
And then, under the general head of Odds and Ends	2,537.50
Making a total disbursement of (*hurriedly*)	$416,546.75

or a net deficit of—ah—several thousand dollars.

Now, these figures bring us down only to October. In October my sister was married, and the house was all torn up, and in the general confusion we lost track of the figures for May and August. All those wishing the *approximate* figures for May and August, however, may obtain them from me in the vestry after the dinner, where I will be with pledge cards for those of you who wish to subscribe over and above your annual dues, and I hope that each and every one of you here tonight will look deep into his heart and (*archly*) into his pocketbook, and see if he can not find it there to help us to put this thing over with a bang (*accompanied by a wholly ineffectual gesture representing a bang*) and to help and make this just the biggest and best year the Armenians have ever had. . . . I thank you.

(*Exits, bumping into proscenium*)

ROBERT BENCHLEY

Mr. Monday, the distinguished evangelist, the best known Protestant Pontiff in America, had once been a prize-fighter. Satan had not dealt justly with him. As a prize-fighter he gained nothing but his crooked nose, his celebrated vocabulary, and his stage-presence. The service of the Lord had been more profitable. He was about to retire with a fortune. It had been well-earned, for, to quote his last report, "Rev. Mr. Monday, the Prophet with a Punch, has shown that he is the world's greatest salesman of salvation, and that by efficient organization the overhead of spiritual degeneration may be kept down to an unprecedented rock-bottom basis. He has converted over two hundred thousand lost and priceless souls at an average cost of less than ten dollars a head. . . .

An expense fund of forty thousand dollars had been underwritten; out on the County Fair Grounds a Mike Monday Tabernacle had been erected, to seat fifteen thousand people. In it the prophet was at this moment concluding his message:

"There's a lot of smart college professors and tea-guzzling slobs in this burg that say I'm a roughneck and a never-wuzzer and my knowledge of history is not-yet. Oh, there's a gang of woolly-whiskered book-lice that think they know more than Almighty God, and prefer a lot of Hun science and smutty German criticism to the straight and simple word of God. Oh, there's a swell bunch of Lizzie boys and lemon-suckers and pie-faces and infidels and beer-bloated scribblers that love to fire off their filthy mouths and yip that Mike Monday is vulgar and full of mush. Those pups are saying now that I hog the gospel show, that I'm in it for the coin. Well, now listen, folks! I'm going to give those birds a chance! They can stand right up here and tell me to my face that I'm a galoot and a liar and a hick! Only if they do—if they do!—don't faint with surprise if some of those rum-dumm liars get one good

206

swift poke from Mike, with all the kick of God's Flaming Righteousness behind the wallop! Well, come on, folks! Who says it? Who says Mike Monday is a four-flush and a yahoo? Huh? Don't I see anybody standing up? Well, there you are! Now I guess the folks in this man's town will quit listening to all this kyoodling from behind the fence; I guess you'll quit listening to the guys that pan and roast and kick and beef, and vomit out filthy atheism; and all of you'll come in, with every grain of pep and reverence you've got, and boost all together for Jesus Christ and his everlasting mercy and tenderness!"

SINCLAIR LEWIS

CHAPTER TEN

Some Cults and O-Cults In Verse

"O bards of rhyme and metre free,
My gratitude goes out to ye
For all your deathless lines—ahem!
Let's see now. . . . What is one of them?

FRANKLIN P. ADAMS

The curfew tolls the knell of parting day,
 The whippoorwill salutes the rising moon,
And wanly glimmer in her gentle ray,
 The sinuous windings of the turbid Spoon.

Here where the flattering and mendacious swarm
 Of lying epitaphs their secrets keep,
At last incapable of further harm
 The lewd forefathers of the village sleep.

The earliest drug of half-awakened morn,
 Cocaine or hashish, strychnine, poppy-seeds
Or fiery produce of fermented corn
 No more shall start them on the day's misdeeds.

For them no more the whetstone's cheerful noise.
 No more the sun upon his daily course
Shall watch them savouring the genial joys,
 Of murder, bigamy, arson and divorce.

Here they all lie; and, as the hour is late,
 O stranger, o'er their tombstones cease to stoop,
But bow thine ear to me and contemplate
 The unexpurgated annals of the group.

There are two hundred only: yet of these
 Some thirty died of drowning in the river,
Sixteen went mad, ten others had D. T.'s.
 And twenty-eight cirrhosis of the liver.

Several by absent-minded friends were shot,
 Still more blew out their own exhausted brains,
One died of a mysterious inward rot,
 Three fell off roofs, and five were hit by trains.

One was harpooned, one gored by a bull-moose,
 Four on the Fourth fell victims to lock-jaw,
Ten in electric chair or hempen noose
 Suffered the last exaction of the law.

Stranger, you quail, and seem inclined to run;
  But, timid stranger, do not be unnerved;
I can assure you that there was not one
  Who got a tithe of what he had deserved.

Full many a vice is born to thrive unseen,
  Full many a crime the world does not discuss,
Full many a pervert lives to reach a green
  Replete old age, and so it was with us.

Here lies a parson who would often make
  Clandestine rendezvous with Claflin's Moll,
And 'neath the druggist's counter creep to take
  A sip of surreptitious alcohol.

And here a doctor, who had seven wives,
  And, fearing this *ménage* might seem grotesque,
Persuaded six of them to spend their lives
  Locked in a drawer of his private desk.

And others here there sleep who, given scope,
  Had writ their names large on the Scrolls of Crime,
Men who, with half a chance, might haply cope,
  With the first miscreants of recorded time.

Doubtless in this neglected spot is laid
  Some village Nero who has missed his due,
Some Bluebeard who dissected many a maid,
  And all for naught, since no one ever knew.

Some poor bucolic Borgia here may rest
  Whose poisons sent whole families to their doom,
Some hayseed Herod who, within his breast,
  Concealed the sites of many an infant's tomb.

Types that the Muse of Masefield might have stirred,
  Or walked to ecstasy Gaboriau,
Each in his narrow cell at last interred,
  All, all are sleeping peacefully below.

. . . . .

Enough, enough! But, stranger, ere we part.
Glancing farewell to each nefarious bier,
This warning I would beg you take to heart,
"There is an end to even the worst career!"

J. C. SQUIRE

If a Very New Poet Had Written "The Lotus Eaters"

I.

Ah!
Ough!
Umph!
It *was* a sweat!
Thank God, that's over!
No more navigating for me
I am on to
Something
Softer . . .
Conductor
Give us a tune!

II.

Work!
Did I used to work?
I seem to remember it
Out there.
Millions of fools are still at
It,
Jumping about
All over the place. . . .
And what's the good of it all? . . .
Buzz,
Hustle,
Pop,
And then . . .
Dump
In the grave.

III.

Bring me six cushions
A yellow one, a green one, a purple one, an orange one,
    an ultramarine one, and a vermilion one,

Colours of which the combination
Pleases my eye.
Bring me
Also
Six lemon squashes
And
A straw. . . .

IV.

I have taken off my coat.
I shall now
Loosen
My braces.

V.

Now I am
All right . . .
My God. . . .
I do feel lazy!

J. C. SQUIRE

(The two verse parodies which follow were part of a successful literary hoax perpetrated by Witter Bynner and Arthur Davison Ficke under the pseudonyms, Anne Knish and Emanuel Morgan. The volume entitled *Spectra* was alleged in the Preface to be a volume of poetic experiments by a group of New Poetry adherents who were advancing far beyond Futuristic Art. Their aim was to speak to the mind of a "process of diffraction by which are disarticulated the several colored and other rays of which light is composed." A poem, they said, "is to be regarded as a prism, upon which the colorless white light of infinite existence falls and is broken up into glowing, beautiful, and intelligible hues." The hoax was sufficiently successful to take in reviewers and critics who made weighty judgments on the volume. It was even parodied!)

"THE FUTILITY OF THINKING"

Her soul was freckled
Like the bald head
Of a jaundiced Jewish banker.
Her fair and featurous face
Writhed like
An albino boa-constrictor.
She thought she resembled the Mona Lisa.
This demonstrates the futility of thinking.

"LIQUOR, LAUGHTER, AND LIMBS"

If I were only dafter
    I might be making hymns
To the liquor of your laughter
    And the laquer of your limbs.

But you turn across the table
    A telescope of eyes,
And it lights a Russian sable
    Running circles in the skies. . . .

Till I go running after,
    Obeying all your whims—
For the liquor of your laughter
    And the laquer of your limbs.

"THE GRACKLE AND THE PEAR TREE"

(Being a Symposium in the manner of certain Modern American Poets
who had been shown a Tree with a Bird on it, and told it was a Grackle.)

RAMBUNCTO

A la Edwin Arlington Robinson

Well, they're quite dead, Rambuncto; thoroughly dead.
It was a natural thing enough; my eyes
Stared baffled down the forest aisles, brown and green,
Not learning what the marks were . . . still, who knows?
Not I, who stooped and picked the things that day,
Scarlet and gold and smooth, friend—smooth enough!
And she's in a vault now, old Jane Fotheringham,
My mother-in-law; and my wife's seven aunts,
And that cursed bird who used to sit and croak
Upon their pear tree . . . they threw scraps to him . . .
My wife, too . . . Lord, that was a curious thing!
Because—"I don't like mushrooms much," I said;
So they ate all I picked. . . . And then they died.
But—well, who knows it isn't better that way?
It's quieter, anyhow. . . . Rambuncto—friend—
Why, you're not going? Well . . . it's a stupid year,
And the world's very useless. . . . Sorry. . . . Still
The dusk intransience that I much prefer
Leaves room for little hope and less regret.
I don't suppose he'd care to stay and dine
Under the circumstances. . . . What's life for?

A la Robert Frost

There was a grackle sat on our old pear tree—
    Don't ask me why; I never did really know;
But he made my wife and me feel for actually the first time
    We were out in the genuine country, hindering things to grow;

It gave us a sort of queer feeling to hear the grackle grackle,
    But when it got to be winter time he rose up and went thence;
And now we shall never know, though we watch the tree till April,
    Whether his curious crying ever made sound or sense.

THE HOBOKEN GRACKLE AND THE HOBO: AN EXPLANATION

A la Vachel Lindsay

As I went marching, torn socked, free, (*Steadily*)
With my red heart marching all agog in front of me,
And my throbbing heels
And my throbbing feet
Making an impression on the Hoboken street, (*With energy*)
Then I saw a pear tree, a fowl, a bird,
And the worst sort of noise an Illinoiser ever heard; (*Disgustedly*)
Banks—of—poets—round—that—tree—
All of the *Po*etry Society but *me!*
All acackle, addressed it as a grackle, (*Chatteringly, as parrots*)
Showed me its hackle (that proved it was a fly)
Tweet, tweet, tweet, tweet! (*Cooingly, yet with annoyance*)
Gosh, what a packed street!
The Secretary, *President,* and TREASURER went by!

"That's not a grackle," says I to all of him,
Seething with their poetry, iron tongued, grim—
"That's an English sparrow on that limb!"

And they all went home
No more to roam,
And I saw their unmade poetry rise up like foam;
And I took my bandanna again on my stick
And walked to a grocery store and took my pick—
I bought crackers, canned shrimps, corn,
Codfish like the flakes of snow at morn,
Buns for breakfast and a fountain pen,
Threw my change down and walked out again,
And I walked through Hoboken, torn socked, free,
WITH MY RED HEART GALUMPHING ALL AGOG IN
    FRONT OF ME!

MARGARET WIDDEMER

Take away the stuff!

Haul it out o' my sight, dump it into the Chicago River, clean the streets with it, let the fat-bellied rich wash down their frogs' legs with it.

I won't traffic with it; it's poison; it drives you crazy; it gives you the D.T.'s and the willies, and I'm not the only one that can prove it—

Not by a damsite; not by a long shot; not by the purple jowels of the brewers and the distillers—God strike 'em dead with their stiff shirts on!

There are ten million wives and widows can prove it; yes, twenty million; thirty million; thirty-seven million; five hundred thousand, in the forty-eight states and some Territories—

And some of the wives have children, and some of the widows have orphans, all legitimate and registered, and entitled to decent treatment, and a fine mess booze has made of them, including those who will grow up to be Presidents of the United States.

Think of them, forty years from now, sitting in the blue room of the White House, recalling their rotten childhoods—spoiled and embittered because their fathers came home blind drunk, smelling like a municipal budget, and raised hell and sang drivelling songs, and fell asleep with their clothes on, anywhere from the sink to the ceiling—

What kind of Presidents do you think they'll make?

Go among the Hunkies, the Wops, the Micks, the Californians— the workers and foreigners, who dig the coal and the ditches and furnish the stuff for the Sunday rotogravure supplements—

I except the Kikes, who prefer gambling and women—

And you'll see what John Barleycorn has put over; you'll get your booze-facts straight from the shoulder, so help me God, you will, I'm telling you till I sweat.

And the same holds for native Americans, as hard drinking a race as ever licked their chops in front of a bar, or in a side-room, or sat down on a curbstone to wait for the cop or Xmas.

I hate the stuff.

When you say saloon, I see red buffaloes charging along the plains
 like a bloody hurricane;
I want to pull the hair out of my chest, and brandish it like a torch
 in the faces of the anti-prohibitionists, the bootleggers, the
 scofflaws, and the big corporations.
Take it out o' my sight; don't tempt me; I wouldn't taste it for the
 stockyards—all right I'll take a swig, but it won't change me,
 mind; I'm agin it!
Cripes! but I'm agin it!

SAMUEL HOFFENSTEIN

And so depart into dark
long in limbo, hornet-stung and following battered flags
and then manufacturing various hells for his own enemies
   all stamped EZRA POUND
    (Phoebus, what a name
      to swill the speaking trump, *gloriae futuris*)
though ole T.S.E. proclaimed his maestro
    and in *such* prose, my God
      constipated but dignified like an elderly cat
"trying his technique so that it will be ready like a well-oiled fire—
engine when the moment comes to strain it to the ut-
most," ooh, my God, *splendeur Dex!*

But the *Criterion* folded
   (good old *Criterion* many a happy hour
   have I spent at the bar watching the lovelies
   shantih
    shantih?
      No, 'e shan't!)
and the cantos went not with a bang but a fizzle
   didn't even get ther ber-luddy reviews
and the expatriate adorers all came running back to mamma's
   womb
so there was no one left to visit the shrine. . . .

We have observed, quoth Plinius, that sacrifices hitherto popular in
many provinces of the empire have now almost ceased, to the great
impoverishment of butchers, graziers, and the like. Dabam Romae
prid. III Kal. Iul.: that's June 1, buddy, in their dago lingo. . . .

And there sat the well-oiled fire-engine
all ready to strain its gutmost
   eek ow ouf honk honk
unable to think, but ready to quote and paraphrase in six languages
including Provencal
   ei didl didl
   li chat e li fidl

it took a man like Ezra to kill Provencal poetry
for us. . . .

And he had learnt all he could
    not a hell of a lot
                —sterile bulls, that was a good one, Canto I
    a significant bit of bull
    Cimbrorumque Minas—Welsh coal mines, meant to be funny,
        maybe?
    pretty damn funny, anyway
    QUAINT like all his Chinese and Greeks and Romans
    they appear QUAINT to Homer Pound's boy from the
        backwoods
The Idaho poeta. . . .

And his temper was never good, you get eccentric living in Rapallo
    and loving
BEAUTY
    the emperor is at Ko
    but No
    silken strings shiver no longer, clashing of smilax, dark nuts
    on the dry bough, nuts on wet earth, nuts
it's lonesome, too, being the only one who understands
                    Caius Properzius,
            'Alkaios,
        Li Pu,
    all great guys,
    an' I *know* 'em, see?
Uncle Ezry on the Acropopopoulos, the rube at the grocery
    stove
    gignetei colon
    :
SO?
So he took to damning his own country, living in Rapallo and Rome*
    among the blackshirted brownbottomed yellowhearted
        Heroes

———————————

* The parody was written just after his treasonous broadcast had begun to hit
us strongly—Author's note.

223

the gallant macaronis that ran from the Greeks, 3 to 1 aera!
aera! !

whoosh! !

----sure, Ezra loved 'em:
the lover of the third-rate loving fascist Italia e l'IMPERO
pfft
the bogus aristocrat wanting Discipline and no Lower
Classes

So Ezra attacked the ole USA and pluto-bolsho-Britain
Jews, & negroes, & Roosevelt, & armament trusts, & usurers
melodious swill-pipe for Goebbels
(Frank Sullivan says Gayda is the only newspaper that
can write the way a Pekinese barks . . . He shd read Ezra's
XIVth Canto. . . . .
tender . . .
like a centaur's asphodel . . .)

And so to his own hell, the last hell, the ninth hell, Antenora
of ice
for traitors
teeth gnashing like the chattering of storks

GILBERT HIGHET

Deflective rhythm under seas
  Where Sappho tuned the snarling air;
A shifting of the spectral lines
  Grown red with gravity and wear.

New systems of coordinates
  Disturb the Sunday table-cloth.
Celestine yawns. Sir Oliver
  Hints of the jaguar and sloth.

A chord of the eleventh shrieks
  And slips beyond the portico.
The night contracts. A warp in space
  Has rumors of Correggio.

Lights. Mrs. Blumenthal expands;
  Calories beyond control.
The rector brightens. Tea is served:
  Euclid supplanted by the sole.

LOUIS UNTERMEYER

(As suggested by Budd Schulberg's novel, *The Disenchanted,* Arthur Mizener's biography, *The Far Side of Paradise,* etc. etc. With the usual apologies to Mr. Eliot.)

Let us go then, you and I,
When Dartmouth is spread out against the sky
Like a student cracked-up on a ski-run.
Oh, damn it, Budd, don't ask, "What is it?"
Let us go and make our visit.

St. Paul bore me. Princeton and Hollywood
Undid me.

Between the conception
And the creation
Falls the Script.

I should have been a pair of shoulder pads
Scatting across the gridiron, beating Yale.

In the dorm the coeds come and go
Talking of Michael Arlen, Bow.

Where are the words that stab, what ideas grow
Out of this academic rubbish?
And the dull class gives no shelter, the library no relief,
And the dry prof no sound of soda water.

Chiantichiantichianti

And when I was a youngster, prepping at Newman,
The coach sent me in to play safety,
And I was frightenend. And out I came.
In one's room with a book, there you feel free.
I drink, much of the night, and go south in the winter.

Perkins is the kindest editor, quarrying
Novels out of Wolfe, mixing Hemingway and Eastman.
And indeed there will be time,
Time for *Esquire* and the *Post,*

Time for *Gatsby* and the *Night*,
And time yet for a hundred indiscretions;
Time for Perkins and revisions.
In the dorm the coeds come and go
Talking of Michael Arlen, Bow.

To Hollywood then I came
Burned out burned out
Twad twad twad
Junk junk junk junk
So couthly forced
Thalberg.

Under the real smog of a California dawn
Here is no art but only tripe
Tripe and no art and Sunset Boulevard
Here one can neither think nor dream nor write
But loud technical mouthing
There is not even silence in the desert
But red sullen faces of cameramen snarl
From platforms on location

I see crowds of extras, walking round a set.
Thank you. If you see Mr. Schulberg, your father,
Tell him I bring the scenario myself:
One must be so careful these days, with budding novelists about.

In the
In the dark
In the dark night of the soul
It's always three o'clock in the morning.

I had not thought death had undone so many.
Then I saw one I knew, and stopped him, crying:
                "Bishop!
"You who were with me on the *Lit* at Nassau!
"That Trilling review you planted last year in *Partisan,*
"Has it begun to sprout? Will it come out this year?
"Or has the editorial frost disturbed its bed?"

No! I am not Prince Hamlet, nor Prince Scott, either,
As Lardner said I was.
I am no Conrad—and in my bibliography there's no great matter;
I have seen the fashion of my Jazz Age flicker,
And I have seen the Nouveau Critic hold my coon-skin coat, and
      snicker,
And in short, I was afraid.
"Am I right or wrong?"
I ask the headwaiter . . .
I smile, of course,
And go on drinking Bushmill's.

I grow old . . . I am knelled . . .
I shall no longer wear the bottoms of my trousers belled.
You will see me any evening in the bar.
As from afar
I remark a classmate assaulted in a speakeasy in New York,
Crawling home to the Princeton Club to die.
Another classmate tumbled from a skyscraper . . .

I remain self-possessed
Except that sometimes there's a ghostly rumble among the drums,
The asthmatic whisper of trombones,
Recalling Carcassonne and proms,

I shall wear my football togs, and walk out upon the field.
I have heard the cheerleaders cheering, each to each.

I do not think that they will cheer for me.

And would it have been worth it, after all,
After the gin, the olive sandwiches,
Among the porcelain,
Would it have been worthwhile,
To have bitten off the Great American Novel,
To have crossed the river, and squatted on my hams under the trees,
To say: "I am Lazarus, Budd, come from the dead,
Come back to show you how, tell you all—tell you all, that's fit
      to print?"

And would it have been worth it, after all,
After the Jelly-Beans and Flappers, after
The scrapbooks and the shawl,
After the Paris night in clusters,
After the cotton bathing trunks, full of the Mediterranean's bright
        heat—
If one, gazing at the figurine,
Or darting hurried glances at the busts of Shakespeare and Galileo,
        should say:
"That is not what I meant, at all,

But at my back from time to time I hear
The horns of Marmons and the sax's wail which shall bring
Scott to Zelda in the spring.

The novel's strand is broken: The Last Tycoon is
Clutched by stronger hands—the Bunny Hug. The tributes
Cross from East to West, unheard. The readers are departed.
Huck's river, run softly, till they end my song.

Mrs. Parker comes at noon.
And then the lighting of the candles
In the William Wordsworth Room.
        Shantih shantih shantih

JOHN ABBOT CLARK

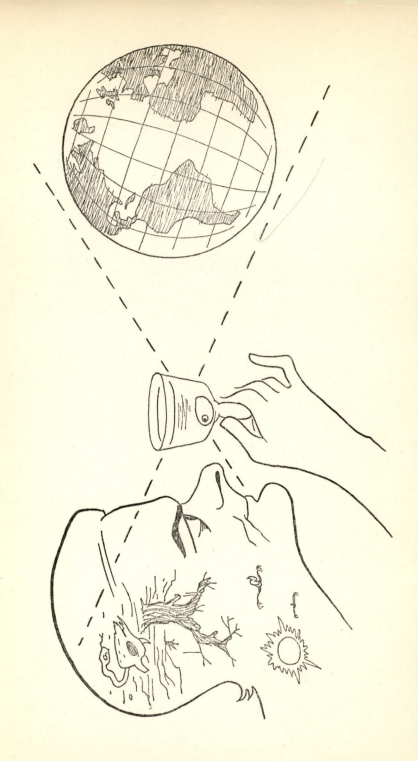

"THE MOIST LAND"

(Being an account of the flight of Mr. T. S. Eliot from Scotland into Shropshire, from Shropshire into Wales, and thence into the Irish Sea.)

Unum, duo, tres, quattuor, quinque, sex, septem, octo, novem, decem; shema yisrael, adonai alohainu adonai echad; nun Wilhelm, wie geht's in der Schule, ganz gut, papa; ibid, infra dig, anon, sic, anno mirabile.

I. The Demobilization of the Fleet

April's very fickle following
March which is very windy, following
February, very sleety, following
December, and so next year is this year
And so forth and so forth and so forth,
Etcetera, und so weiter.

The Archduke in scarlet hunting coat came down to breakfast
Having slept all night with his hunting-boots under the sheets
His gun by his side. The steel of the barrel glittered
All night like phosphorescence in the room heavy with panatellas.
"Officer, which way is uptown, and if so which way is downtown?
I am a widow woman from Lynn, Massachusetts, and have never
       been here before.
Though I have a cousin on the force whose name is Sweeney,
A Titanic fellow, big I mean, bronzed as iodine,
Do you know him perhaps?
Perhaps, perchance, haply, mayhap, maybe?
Yes, no, nein, ja, oui, si, non?"
"My own name is Schulz. No Sweeney do I know."
"And yet my own husband was German. I am as I said a widow
       woman."

In Hamburg an der Elbe
Da schwimmt ein Krokodil.

Now gleam the birches ghost-white wherever they are.
The sacerdotal poplars seem to have taken off their surplices

Against the heat. What time is it, Nathan?
Quelle heure est-il? Or is the Big Ben out of order again?
The perch season is open in eastern West Virginia,
Give me a silver arrow and a bow of polished tin,
Give me a cross-bow out of Thessaly or Irkutsk,
Or an old-fashioned Winchester such as pawnbrokers still use in
       Erie, Pa., against burglars,
And I will prick their shins in the delicate mine-water,
The dirty perch!
How long, oh, Catiline, will you keep up this pish-posh?

Come, Marie, let us go to the Moscow Art Theatre.
Zhil ya na Tiflise
Bil ya na Kavkase.
Closer, Marie (is not that Mischa Elman going into the shop to
       buy rosin—
He is a short fellow for his height, don't you think?)
Come closer, and we shall watch the moon rise over Tammany Hall.
The violins begin, let us imagine they are nightingales,
Singing their last, for the world ends tomorrow.
(About this time the fat-legged chorus comes on; do they still say,
       "So this is Paris?")
Come, we will stand on the corner of Fourteenth Street and Third
       Avenue.
The world is falling about us like a whole autumn;
Come close, in the shadow, in the shadow,
The shadow that lengthens and lengthens,
As if we stood under the legs of a Colossus.
My heart is broken, Marie; the moon is red
With blood. And I wonder, I wonder,
Which six of the seven cities that claimed Homer were liars?
Comment allez-vous? Très bien, Monsieur.

II. A Three-Handed Game of Pinochle

Antiques, Madame? The Modern Antique Company
Has been in business forty-seven years
And never one dissatisfied customer.
Benvenuto! Benvenuto Cellini!

Tarry a moment, it is I, Fra Lippo Lippi,
There are two damsels in the cemetery
Waiting for us under the cypresses;
Let's go together.
Chi troppo sale
Precipitevolissimevolmente.
Flow softly, Wabash, till I end my song!
"Oh, God, how I hate things out of Grand Rapids!"
Have you ever known what it is to hunger for objets d'art?
This candelabra, *par exemple,* pray
Examine it; observe this little stain—
This little copper stain—well, it was blood.
"Do you remember the Marchesa—
The fiery little woman out of Bologna?
No? Well, we'll say no more about it!"
"Have you ever been lost in the Schwarzwald, Amalie,
With nothing to eat but those filthy little sausages
They sell in Köln at Schimmel's there on the corner?"

"What was that?"

      "I shouldn't be surprised
If dead men tell no tales."
"I think we've been dead a hundred thousand years."

"Yes, and I know that was Little Red Riding Hood
I saw today on Fort Washington Avenue."
Aloha! Aloha!
But the barges spread sail down the river like peacocks,
Their canopies of orange and azure,
A sailor from Smyrna with a lemon between his teeth
Fell into the water. O there, Demetrios!
"I think you got a nerve, Mr. Rosenzweig, to ask I should marry
        your daughter without a dowry."
In Hongkong I met Kwong Chu,
A mandarin with fingernails a yard long.
He had the most exquisite manners,
And I shall never forget his beautiful angel's smile
When he had us to tea that afternoon in January,

An hour after he had decapitated his mother.
Flow gently, Wabash, till I end my song.
IT'S A QUARTER TO FOUR!
"Is you comin', Andrew Jackson?"
"I ain't sayin' as I ain't."
"I ain't askin' yuh as you ain't; I'se askin' you as yuh is.
Now is yuh?"
IT'S A QUARTER TO FOUR.

Have you met Nastasia Fillipovna, I said,
And he said he hadn't, so I asked him to.
And that was the beginning. She was one
Of those fierce Russian women, knows no fun.
Hurry up, Johnny, and get your gun.
Well, in a week the man was done for.
IT'S A QUARTER TO FOUR.
Good-night, ladies,
Good-night, ladies,
Good-night, ladies,
We're going to leave you now.

By the way, I'm sure you know the *Côte d'azur*.
IT'S A QUARTER TO FOUR.
As for me, I never took anything stronger
Than a thimbleful of rum
Even in the good old days,
But you, Mr. O'Brien, say you drink hair-tonic.
Flow softly, Wabash, till I end my song.
I am the same, Panthides,
I, Leotychides, who once in Elymais
Herded black sheep and by Hypanis shore,
Looking on Thebes a thousand leagues away,
Wreathed for your head a crown of eglantine,
And drank a copper keg of home-made wine.

Hula, hula,
Hula, hula,
Old Mother Hubbard she made my bed.
But what good is it

Since Ivan the Terrible
The Brooklyn Bridge
And Staten Island
Fell on my head?

Oh, Carthage, Carthage,
What boots it that the hawthorns keep their snows
Against these many months of wind and sun?
I resolved to take only sarsaparilla,
But what good did that do?
The clerk dished me up a vanilla,
Believing Columbus a Jew.

Take these, *les fleurs mourantes, mademoiselle.*
There's nothing more for me to say,
(Oh, Neptune, Neptune, call your mermaids in!)
Until you get my letter.
But I know
(*Oi, weh is mir, weh is mir!*)
That they've christened
Petrograd
Something or other,
And there's nothing to do
Until somebody
Can find my brother.
The more's the pity,
He's gone, he's gone
In a Spanish galleon
With Henry VIII
To Atlantic City.

La, la,
I've waited in High Bridge,
But I'm going now.

Rome is burning,
Yes, burning,
Gott
im
Himmel,

burning,
burning,
hula, hula,
la, la.

IV. Thunder and Lightning

The dead are living
And the living are dead
And there's no use giving
Your board and your bed
To the sorrowful woman who came
From Lithuania
Latvia
Vienna or Rumania
Rome or Czecho-Slovakia
With an instep and eyebrows of flame.
Waiki, waiki.
What if I have three keys to my apartment
One gold, one silver, and one lead
Here in this desert place the frogs are withered
The griffons are no bigger than fleas,
The sands are rocky and the rocks are sandy,
And there's not enough water
And not enough brandy
To wash the ears of King Cole's daughter.
Co co lo co po co.
     Of if there were
Oh if there were
     Oh if there were
Do do do do do do
Ra mi fa so.

Let her sit at her piano and play Tschaikowsky,
But we know how black the sun can be
Yom Kippur Eve or when there is no sun at all
We'll wait in this dead land and see
The Woolworth Building fall.

They will be here presently
And we shall be parched and shrivelled,

Whoever they are we shall be blanched and withered.
We have only to say coo coo
And all will be over.
Even the unicorns stay in their dry holes
The vampires mourn. Wait till the thunder speaks
Dada, goo goo
Abracadabra.
My friend you see me dead and yet I know
I have not long to live
After the purple gnats with bovine faces
After Jerusalem's fallen and Mrs. Grundy
Comes by on a black horse with the three graces.
Gautama's gone, the sacred bull is gone.
Apis is gone
Adio, bella Napoli, adio
Adio
Wait Khiva till the Ganges turns to milk,
You'll hear the tiger laugh with green grimaces
You'll see the thunder lift the Himalayas
As if they were a toothpick.
Da da ma ma pa pa
HALLELUJAH
I'll wait awhile for Julian the Apostate
You go and pick the fallen lightnings up
And see if Mrs. Porter
Has got enough soda water.

Farewell, I've turned the prow to Greece again.
Shall I call up my lawyer, Cortland 0004
And say the sea is beautiful tonight.
Brooklyn Bridge is falling down falling down falling down

Amo amas amat amabo amabimus
Huius huius huius—O mea culpa
There's never anything to say though I should say
The less the more. The blue parrot's fainted.
God bless you all. Paracelsus is drunk again.
Daddy. Damdaddy, Damdaddy

Shanty shanty shanty.   SAMUEL HOFFENSTEIN

"EDGAR A. GUEST"

(Considers "The Old Woman Who Lived in a Shoe" and
the Good Old Verities at the Same Time.)

It takes a heap o' children to make a home that's true,
And home can be a palace grand or just a plain, old shoe;
But if it has a mother dear and a good old dad or two,
Why, that's the sort of good old home for good old me and you.

Of all the institutions this side the Vale of Rest
Howe'er it be it seems to me a good old mother's best;
And fathers are a blessing, too, they give the place a tone;
In fact each child should try and have some parents of his own.

The food can be quite simple; just a sop of milk and bread
Are plenty when the kiddies know it's time to go to bed.
And every little sleepy-head will dream about the day
When he can go to work because a Man's Work is his Play.

And, oh, how sweet his life will seem, with nought to make him
cross
And he will never watch the clock and always mind the boss.
And when he thinks (as may occur), this thought will please him
best:
That ninety million think the same—including Eddie Guest.

LOUIS UNTERMEYER

CHAPTER ELEVEN

The Lost (And Found) Generation

"I was sitting at a table at the edge of the arena, sipping *Anis del Toro,* and Hemingway was in the center of the ring, under the lights, fighting a bull. As he flung open his dialogue with both hands, the bull charged, tail up. Hemingway swung his plot clear and, as the bull recharged, brought around his dialogue in a half-circle that pulled the bull to his knees. We all applauded."

COREY FORD

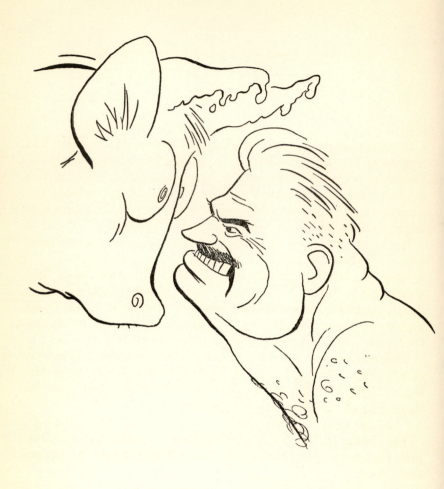

A Mere Boy stood on a pile of blue stones. His attitude was regardant. The day was seal brown. There was a vermilion valley containing a church. The church's steeple aspired strenuously in a direction tangent to the earth's center. A pale wind mentioned tremendous facts under its breath with certain effort at concealment to seven not-dwarfed on an un-distant mauve hilltop.

The Mere Boy was a brilliant blue color. The effect of the scene was not un-kaleidoscopic.

After a certain appreciable duration of time the Mere Boy abandoned his regardant demeanor. The strenuously aspiring church steeple no longer projected itself upon his consciousness. He found means to remove himself from the pile of blue stones. He set his face valleyward. He proceeded.

The road was raw umber. There were in it wagon ruts. There were in it pebbles, Naples yellow in color. One was green. The Mere Boy allowed the idea of the green pebble to nick itself into the sharp edge of the disc of his Perception.

"Ah," he said, "a green pebble."

The rather pallid wind communicated another Incomprehensible Fact to the paranthine trees. It would appear that the poplars understood.

"Ah," repeated the Mere Boy, "a Green Pebble."

"Sh-o," remarked the wind.

The Mere Boy moved appreciably forward. If there were a thousand men in a procession and nine hundred and ninety-nine should suddenly expire, the one man who was remnant would assume the responsibility of the procession.

The Mere Boy was an abbreviated procession.

The blue Mere Boy transported himself diagonally athwart the larger landscape, printed in four colors, like a poster.

On the uplands were chequered squares made by fields, tilled and otherwise. Cloud-shadows moved from square to square. It was as if the Sky and Earth were playing a tremendous game of chess.

By and by the Mere Boy observed an Army of a Million Men. Certain cannon, like voluble but non-committal toads with hunched backs, fulminated vast hiccoughs at unimpassioned intervals. Their own invulnerableness was offensive.

An officer of blue serge waved a sword, like a picture in a school history. The non-committal toads pullulated with brief red pimples and swiftly relapsed to impassivity.

The line of the Army of a Million Men obnubilated itself in whiteness as a line of writing is blotted with a new blotter.

"Go teh blazes b'Jimminey," remarked the Mere Boy. "What yeh's shooting fur? They might be people in that field."

He was terrific in his denunciation of such negligence. He debated the question of his ir-removability.

"If I'm goin' teh be shot," he observed; "If I'm goin' teh be shot, b'Jimminey—"

*　　*　　*

A Thing lay in the little hollow.

The little hollow was green.

The Thing was pulpy white. Its eyes were white. It had blackish-yellow lips. It was beautifully spotted with red, like tomato stains on a rolled napkin.

The yellow sun was dropping on the green plain of the earth, like a twenty-dollar gold piece falling on the baize cloth of a gaming table.

The blue serge officer abruptly discovered the punctured Thing in the Hollow. He was struck with the ir-remediableness of the business.

"Gee," he murmured with interest. "Gee, it's a Mere Boy."

The Mere Boy had been struck with seventy-seven rifle bullets. Seventy had struck him in the chest, seven in the head. He bore close resemblance to the top of a pepper castor.

He was dead.

He was obsolete.

As the blue serge officer bent over him he became aware of a something in the Thing's hand.

It was a green pebble.

"Gee," exclaimed the blue serge officer. "A green pebble, gee."

The large Wind evolved a threnody with reference to the seven un-distant poplars.

FRANK NORRIS

My next dramatic work will be a sextilogy, so called because it will consist of six plays all filled with sex. The acting of it will require fifteen hours. There will be twenty-four different kinds of sex in it, an all-time record. Of these, seven are completely new and have never before appeared in any dramatic work not written by Earl Carroll. Of the seven, six were discovered last spring (in the love season) by the Sullivan-National Geographic Society Expedition to the summit of Havelock Ellis. The seventh is a new, rustproof, non-collapsible kind of sex, invented by myself after years of research during my odd moments; moments which grew odder and odder as my investigations progressed. This new variety of sex is made from goldenrod, and I call it Tooralooraluminum.

The sextilogy will concern the goings-on of a family named Baddun. The family consists of a Confederate veteran, General Baddun, who is hated by his wife, Alla Baddun, who in turn is loved by their son, Earle Baddun, and hated by their daughter, Alice Baddun, who is in love with her father and her brother.

As the sextilogy opens, the Badduns are discovered having a snack of breakfast consisting of creamed henbane, toadstools, *sous-cloche,* and Paris-green pudding with strychnine sauce. A percolator of Prussic acid bubbles cozily on the range. The favors are special suicide revolvers which, by simply pulling the trigger, can also be used for murdering one's next of kin.

The Badduns sit there glowering at each other. Earle is staring at Alice. Alice shudders, and buries her face in a remote part of her hands, where she thinks Earle will never find it.

EARLE—Nice weather we're having.
ALICE (*sternly*)—Earle!
EARLE—What?
ALICE—Why do you say that? You know it's not nice weather we're having. It may be nice weather for others, but it can never

be nice weather for us Badduns. Why do you look at me like that, Earle, with desire in your elms? For God's sake, stop looking at me like that, Earle! Don't touch me, Earle!

EARLE—All right, I won't—if you incest.

ALLA—Life is just a bowl of cherries.

EARLE—Mother, may I be excused from table?

ALLA—Why, my son?

EARLE—I want to shoot myself. I'll only be gone a minute.

ALLA—But why do you want to shoot yourself, my boy?

EARLE—It's all so horrible, Mother.

ALLA—What's horrible, dear?

EARLE—Life, Mother, Life. When I was in the army, every mother I shot seemed to look like every other mother I shot, and every mother looked like you, Mother. And then every other mother began to look like me, Mother, and I felt that every time I killed somebody's mother I was committing suicide and every time I committed suicide I felt I looked like every other Eugene O'Neill.

ALLA—Life is just a bowl of Eugene O'Neills.

EARLE—Oh, never leave me, Mother. You and I will go away together, away from all this, far away. I know an island in the Pacific—

GENERAL BADDUN (*eagerly*)—Say, is it a little short island about seventeen miles in circumference, with palm trees all over it?

EARLE—Yes, and a cliff at the southern extremity.

GENERAL—That's the one! I know that island.

EARLE—You *do!*

GENERAL—I'll say I do! Boy, if it could talk, the stories that island could tell about me!

EARLE—It's certainly a small world.

ALICE (*shuddering*)—It's a horrible world. . . . Mother!

ALLA—What?

ALICE—Stop looking at father like that. Father!

GENERAL—What?

ALICE—Stop looking at Mother like that. Earle!

EARLE—What?

ALICE—Stop looking at me like that.

EARLE—Alice!

ALICE—What?

EARLE—Stop looking at father like that. And, Dr. Joseph Collins, you stop looking at Love and Life like that.

ALLA—Life is a bowl of Dr. Joseph Collinses.

GENERAL—May I have another cup of Prussic acid, Alla? Two lumps please. . . . Thanks. My, I always say there's nothing like a cup of good strong, black prussic acid to wake you up in the morning and clear the brain of cobwebs. Alla, are you still being unfaithful to me with that ship captain?

ALLA—Which one, dear?

GENERAL—You know—the one that's my step-cousin or something.

ALLA—I thi-ink so, but I'm not sure. You know my memory. What's his name?

GENERAL—Brump. Captain Adam Brump.

(*Alla takes an address book from her crinoline and consults it.*)

ALLA—Let me see-ee—Bradge, Braim, Brattigan, Brelk, Briffel, Broskowitz—yes, here he is. Brump. Captain Adam Brump. But why do you ask about him, dear. Anything wrong with him?

GENERAL—No, no! Fine fellow. Go right ahead. Have a good time. You're only young once.

ALICE (*gloomily*)—It's not so. We Badduns are always Jung.

ALLA—Life gets Adler and Adler.

EARLE—Oh, Mother dear, I'm afreud, I'm so afreud. Let us go to my island in the Pacific.

(*Alice shudders*)

ALLA—General, I wish you'd speak to Alice about this constant shuddering. She'll have the plaster shuddered off half the rooms in the house if she doesn't quit.

(*Enter Norn, a maid.*)

NORN—The coffin man is here, sir.

GENERAL—Tell him we don't want any today.

EARLE—Oh, we don't, don't we!

(*Earle draws a revolver and shoots his father.*)

NORN—(*shouting downstairs to the coffin man*)—One on the coffin, Joe.

249

(*From below, like an echo of the voice of the tragic and relentless Fate that pursues the Badduns, floats the answering voice of the coffin man: "O.K."*)

EARLE—I'm not sorry I shot Father. He looked like a Philadelphia postman.

ALLA—Life is a Philadelphia postman—slow, gray, inexorable.

ALICE—Life is a bag of mail. And death—death is a canceled stamp.

EARLE—Birth is a special delivery.

ALICE—Better we Badduns had never been born. Here, Earle. Here is a cigar.

EARLE—Why do you give me a cigar, Alice?

ALICE—For scoring a bulls-eye on Father, Earle. Does anybody else wish to take a chance? Step right up, folks . . .

EARLE—Cigars. When I was in the army, every cigar I smoked looked like every other cigar. Every time I smoked a cigar I felt I was committing suicide.

ALICE—I shall go mad.

ALLA—You will go mad.

EARLE—She will go mad.

AUDIENCE—We shall go mad.

EARLE—You will go mad.

EUGENE O'NEILL—They will go mad.

EARLE (*turning quickly to O'Neill*)—Are you Eugene O'Neill, the playwright?

GENE—To put it mildly, Son.

ALLA—Give him the works, Earle.

ALICE—Yes, give it to him, Earle. See how *he* likes being bumped off.

EARLE—Mr. O'Neill, on behalf of those members of the casts of your recent plays who have not died like flies from overwork, it gives me great pleasure to plug you with this thirty-eight calibre—

GENE—But—

ALLA—What is Life, Gene, but one great big But?

(*Earle shoots Gene.*)

ALICE—Now, come on. Let's boil this thing down to three acts.

ALLA—One act, or I won't commit suicide.

ALICE—All right, one it is. Get up, Father. Snap out of that coffin.

FRANK SULLIVAN

Chapter I

The city of Grand Revenant, in High Hope County and the sovereign state of Nostalgia, has a population of 34,567, according to the official census taker, a vast and bumbling liar, receiver of puny bribes and secret high acolyte of the poems of Algernon Charles Swinburne.

Grand Revenant is 49.6 miles from Zenith and 99.2 from Gopher Prairie.

It was founded in 1903, a year that also saw the birth, at Kitty Hawk, N. C., of a strange boxlike contrivance that held the bright seeds of death for Coventry and Nagasaki and other proud cities half the world away.

Its pioneer settler was old Cornelius Ampersand, a prodigious seducer of Indians along the thundering marge of Lake Prolix and on the cold, improbable trails that lead from Baedeker and Larousse to Mount Thesaurus. Corn was a He-Man, a Wowser, a High Annointed Member of the Sacred and Splendiferous Tribe of Good Scouts, and if his thin, despairing wife often wept alone in the night, nobody knew—except perhaps her two or three hundred closest friends.

In the years since old Corn raped his last squaw (and how those golden girls would giggle in the dusk!), Grand Revenant had grown like an angry weed in the fertile soil of the prairie.

Factories came—Wilson and Fadiman, who ravaged the little firm-breasted hills for copper for moot points; Trilling and Cowley, who made the smoothest, shiniest, most astoundingly complicated little instruments for determining tension and slack (it was hard to say what everybody did before it was possible to determine slack to one-thousandth part of an inch); Mencken & Nathan, who manufactured Hortex and were said to have the seventh largest mangle in the state of Nostalgia.

Stores were born—the Mad Mode Mart, Avis Cormorant, prop. (Miss Cormorant was a nymphomaniac and, very discreetly, a German spy, but her chic was the despair of her rival, Elsie Drear, who was a virgin and an Episcopalian); Blitberg's Department Store ("Nous l'Avons!"), which sold everything from needles to yachts, and if one or two salesgirls died each week from a strange and terrible disease called Dreiser's Botch, there was surely no kinder or merrier man in all Revenant than old Sam Blitberg; Dirge and Mouseman (Mrs. Mouseman, nee Birdie Jump, was that object of almost inconceivable grandeur, a former inmate of the *Social Register*), where you could buy, for very little more than it would cost to build supernal beauty or to stamp out Yaws, rare stones of devious and bloody history.

Other noble monuments—the Revenant Museum of Art, which boasted a Modigliani and a Dali and a whole roomful of Grant Woods, but which was chiefly notable for its swimming pool which was as deep and blue as a lake; Revenant Junior High School, which regularly and gratifyingly beat the up-start team from East Hemingway in the annual marathon, and if very few of her graduates could tell you who wrote "Thanatopsis" or even "Mantrap," they usually proved astonishingly nimble at selling not too aqueous real estate and beautifully shiny automobiles, which often ran quite well; and, always and most particularly, Mme. Moriarity's bowling parlors, where the nickering males of Revenant betook themselves for curious delights, which sometimes they even actually enjoyed.

Churches sprang up, to the glory of a Fat God, whose other names were Baal and Moloch and Ahriman and Samuel and Progress and Rugged Individualism.

Hotels and restaurants—the Revenant Inn, which travellers had been known to compare favorably with the glittering Bellevue-Stratford in Philadelphia, but at which there was no room for the Indians whose doomed camp-fires had once glowed where now its flying towers mocked the sky; Doung's Hotburger, where the cop on the beat, a cold and melancholy man, dropped in nightly to sigh: "Geez, you take my wife. A good woman, I guess, but no get-up-

and-go to her like some of these peppy society dames. And *talk!* Golly! One of these days maybe I'll have to shut the ole girl up." At six o'clock one bitter January morning, he did, very neatly and irrevocably, using the old .44 service revolver with which he had sworn to uphold the law; the Heyday Grille, where Doc Kennicott and George Babbitt and Sam Dodsworth and all the glorious he-male company of competent seducers (about once a year, Babbitt conducted a fumbling, inconclusive experiment with some derisive young woman in a canoe) and two-fisted drinkers (sometimes, un-easily, they had a cocktail before lunch) met every Friday to bumble cheerfully: "Well, I dunno what you other, uh, homo sapiensibuses think, but it strikes this not so humble observer that this lil ole burg is sure goin' straight to the twenty-three skiddoos." Solemnly, they agreed that Grand Revenant could not compare in splendor with Zenith and Gopher Prairie and Paris and New York; secretly they knew that she was strange and beautiful beyond all other cities of the earth.

Chapter II

Shad Ampersand, old Corn's grandson, lived in a neat $26,500 bungalow called Christmas Past, on Revenant Heights, overlooking the brisk, aspiring town. He was a tall, ramshackle, hayrick of a man of fifty-six, copper-red (a testimony, it was whispered, to old Corn's prowess with the squaws) and sad of eye, like a water spaniel or an early Donatello. An admirer of loneliness and rye whiskey and thin, hawk-vivid girls, who listened with vast polite-ness while he explained such recondite matters as Arbitrary Micro-cosm, Limited Frame of Reference, Elementary Symbolism, and Dated or Synthetic Idiom, about all of which they knew precisely nothing and most enthusiastically cared even less.

Sitting on his tiny porch on one of the brightest, briefest, and most poignant of all October afternoons, Shad was very weightily considering the profound mystery of Sex.

"I'm not one of these highbrow geezers like W. Somerset Maugham or John Q. Galsworthy," he pondered heavily, "and it sure gives me a pain in the old bazookus to hear some long-haired so-called intellectual claiming that love and marriage and kiddies and every-

253

thing a dumb ole roughneck like me has come to hold most sacred is nothing more nor less than something called the Biological Urge."

"Hey, you don't have to talk to *me* like that," said Trenda Boneside sharply. "I'm not the Pulitzer Prize Committee."

She was a small, fierce kitten of a girl, who had lived for nineteen eager, sniffing years with her parents on a farm in Remnant, just across the state line.

"M? Nope. See what you mean," he said placatingly. She was a passionate white flame on a cigar-store lighter. He tried to imagine her cooking his breakfast. Tried and most conspicuously failed.

"No, you don't at all," she snapped at him, this brisk fox terrier of a girl. "You listen to me, Shad Ampersand. I'm not one of those old girls of yours—Carol or Leona or that awful Dodsworth woman, whatever *her* name was."

"Fran," he said humbly.

"Fran. Well, anyway. I'm not. Maybe that old hillbilly talk was all right for them, and even the *American Mercury*. But with me you can just talk like anybody else."

"M."

"That's another thing!" she cried furiously. "That 'M'! What the hell is that supposed to be? The name of a moving picture?"

"Gee, Tren," he sighed. "It's only an experiment in phonetics. You know, how to get something down the way it really sounds. As I was telling ole Doc Bongflap . . ."

Now she was really a tigress.

" 'Bongflap,' " she wailed. "I've known you for a long time, Shad Ampersand, and I've certainly heard some terrible names—Vergil Gunch and Roscoe Geake and Adelbert Shoop—but that's the worst ever. Nobody in the world was ever called Bongflap."

"Well, maybe not, but, drat it, when an author wants to suggest how a character . . ."

"I know all about that," she said, "and I know all about Charles Dickens, too, and you both make me sick. My God, even *Tarkington* wouldn't call anybody Bongflap. Or Timberlane either, for that matter. Timber*lane*. Timber*line*. Even Hansen and Chamberlain ought to be able to get that one, but I think it stinks. I keep thinking it's Tamberlane, or Timberleg."

"Aren't we getting a little off the subject, Tren?" he said mildly.

"I don't know. What *was* the subject?"

"Well, uh, love."

"Oh, *that,*" she yawned. "What about it?"

"Well, uh," he fumbled. She was a laughing brook of a girl, cool, diamond-bright, a wanderer in secret loveliness. He dreamed of her in a gingham apron, cooking his breakfast. Golly! "Uh, I thought we might get married," he whinnied. It was so perhaps that Paris whispered to Helen before they came to the city of the Topless Towers, so the Roman gave his soul to Egypt's queen on the dreaming bosom of the Nile. She looked at him, and suddenly her heart was in her eyes.

"Shad!" she cried, and now she was a bell.

"Wife!" he clamored through their urgent kiss, and miraculously it was a word in nowise stained with use.

Chapter III

The little orange cat called Pox stretched langorously in Shad Ampersand's lap.

"I know you're lonely since your wife, Trenda, left you last November to join Blight Grimes, the polo player and nimble seducer at his hotel in Chicago, Illinois," she mewed. She was a very fetching device of a cat, an explanatory butler at curtain rise in a Lonsdale comedy.

Shad scratched her ears and thought: I should have known all along about Tren and Blight. The time they went away together for a week back in March and Trenda said—oh, she was very innocent and airy about it!—that they'd just gone up to Alaska to look at polo ponies; the time I found them upstairs in bed and they said they were just lying down because their feet hurt. I must have been pretty credulous, he decided, and Pox blinked her copper eyes in sardonic agreement.

"You're damn right," she purred, "but now, of course, she has delerium tremens and this Grimes character isn't exactly the kind of man you can picture running up and down stairs with paraldehyde and strait jackets. There's a strange streak of cruelty in him."

He nodded, but he was thinking despairingly: I must have failed her somehow. Maybe I was wrong to want to keep her here in Christmas Past pasting up scrapbooks for an old galoot like me—Blight, doggone his hide, was only forty-nine and lithe and puissant as a sword—when she ought to be running around with kids her own age, going to the movies and coming out with her head all full of stars and dreams (as a matter of fact, he knew she loathed the movies), having a soda with the gang at Bleeck's and feeding nickels into that juke box for "Smiles" and "Margie," maybe even being kissed, in sweet and childish innocence, in the back seat of a Chevrolet.

"Pope Hartford," said Pox, who was also a mind-reader.

"M?"

"Pope Hartford," repeated the cat irritably. "You might as well stick to the period. And while I think of it, you can lay off that 'M' with *me, too.*"

Anyway, he had failed her, his lost and golden girl, and she was in Chicago with Blight. He looked at his watch. 11:46. Probably they were back from the theater now and up in their suite and Blight was slipping the little silver fox cape from her shoulders.

"His heart contracted," murmured Pox.

"M, uh, I mean what?"

"Don't keep making me say everything twice, for God's sake. 'His heart contracted.' That goes in somewhere. In parentheses. After the second 'and,' I should say. It's one of your mannerisms, though not a very fortunate one. Also you seem to have forgotten that she's on the sauce, if you'll pardon the expression."

Trenda spifflicated, swizzled, tiddly. He knew it was the truth, but the thought was a sharp agony, an unthinkable desecration, as if he saw the slender terrible beauty of the Samothrace deep in foul mud and marred with the droppings of obscene and dreadful birds.

"I think you're overreaching yourself there," said Pox. "Too many modifiers, and it's a pretty elaborate image. After all, you aren't Henry James."

"Golly, Pox—"

"Ah, the hell with it. Let it go. It's your stream of consciousness, thank God, not mine."

In his despair, his cold unutterable loss, Shad Ampersand began to think of all the world, and Pox looked at him sharply for a moment and then hopped off his lap and left the room. Shad thought: Marriage. A man and a woman—him and Tren, Romeo and Juliet, Philemon and Baucis, Ruth and, and, drat it, who *was* that guy—anyway they fell in love—oh, Tren, sweet, we must have been in love the night we read "Gideon Planish" until the stars went out!—and they promised to love, honor, and obey—golly, the most beautiful words in the English language, except, of course, maybe some parts of Shakespeare—till death you did part. But then something happened. One day they woke up and the magic was gone. (He and Tren were having breakfast, Homogenized Virtex and Spookies, and suddenly, appallingly she cried, "Shad!" I'm going away with Blight! Right this minute! He's going to take me to London, Paris, Berlin—Gee I've always wanted to see the Taj Mahal and all those cute little Androgynes or whatever you call 'em—and we're going to take along a sleeping bag, you know, like in that book I read some of, and camp right out on the biggest darn ole Alp we can find." He had burbled, "Gee, that sounds mighty interesting, Tren. Yes, sir. Like to take a little trip sometime myself," but the Spookies were ashes in his mouth.) Anyway, it always ended—either in the hideous, clinging slime of the divorce court, or else—and this was unutterably worse—in the terrible, icy vacuum of indifference, the final shameful acceptance of infidelity. ("You ought to get yourself a girl, Shad," she had told him one night; as usual she was sitting on Blight's lap, knitting a new-fangled sock. "Why don't you call up Avis Cormorant? *There's* a cheerful little giver for you. Or maybe one of those Piutes you say old Corn was always talking about." He had almost struck her then.) It was this, this modern cynicism, this flat denial of marriage, not the Communists or the Fascists or the Technocrats or even the hot-eyed disciples of Fourier and Adam Smith, that was destroying America. In the ultimate scheme of things, the continuing marriage of Tren and Shad Ampersand, or, if you chose, of plain Helen and Robert Lynd, was more important than—

"Hey," said Pox, putting his head around the door, "I wouldn't disturb you, except you didn't seem to be getting anywhere in particular with that editorial. Anyway, she's back."

"Who?" spurted Shad, though his heart obliteratingly knew.

257

"Who the hell did you think?" said Pox scornfully. "Little Round Heels. With a hangover I could swing on by my tail."

She came in then, with a glad, unsteady rush, a broken cry into his waiting arms, and if she was damaged, if she was no longer the bright, imperious child his dreams had known, but something harder, wiser, and infinitely sad, he had no eyes to see.

"Tren, baby!" he whispered fiercely in her hair.

"Shad!" she breathed, and gave him the ruined glory of her smile. After all, she thought, stroking the remembered kindness of his cheek, you always have to figure that the old skeesix is practically indestructible, there ought to be plenty of books still batting around in him for all the endless years to come.

"Nice going, sister," murmured Pox, and most discreetly shut the door.

WOLCOTT GIBBS.

(A Brief Grapple with the Boston Legend After Reading the Complete Works of Mr. J. P. Marquand on the Subject.)

Chapter I

Grindle Point was always best in the fall. If I knew how to write, I could tell how the old river went dreaming by in the sun and how the copper beeches marched down to its bank in strict and orderly procession. Sometimes in the morning, before the mist had burned away, the trees looked like silver ghosts and there were diamonds in the grass on the lawn. Time itself seemed to hang suspended in that clear, level light, so it was easy to believe that all the people who had once lived there were there still and always would be. As I've said, however, I am not a writer, and all I know is that I am part of Grindle Point. It is where I belong.

I shall never forget the day I came back to it after the war. My father was in his study, reading the *Transcript* and eating an apple, as he always did in the later afternoon.

"Hello," he said. "Kill any Germans?"

"Eight or nine," I said. "Nothing to amount to much."

"I suppose not," he said. "Naturally you were decorated?"

"Well, yes," I said. I hadn't meant to tell anybody about the medal, because there is nothing worse than showing off. I only hoped he wouldn't mention it to the servants.

"You look older," he said. "Probably time you were thinking of getting married."

"I don't know," I said. "I've never been much good at that kind of thing."

"An awkward business," said my father. "Going off that way with a comparatively strange woman."

I could see he was embarrassed. He wanted to tell me something, but it was hard because we had never talked together very freely.

"A damned awkward business," he repeated irritably. "They ought to have told you about it at Harvard. I suppose it's customary these days to assume that a gentleman knows about these things instinctively, but sometimes he doesn't."

"Yes, sir," I said.

"All a man can do is try to play the game," he said. "It won't be easy, especially with your training, but the Apleys have always got through it somehow. With me it was always something one owed to Harvard. A matter of loyalty."

I could understand that. Harvard had made me what I was, and the least I could do in return was to make a certain amount of effort.

"I'll do my best, sir," I said.

Just the same, I wasn't happy when I got up to my old room and started unpacking my bag. Outside my window the river lay opalescent in the twilight, but for a moment I saw it as a dark and relentless torrent bearing me on into the unknowable future, and I shuddered. I didn't want to get married; I just wanted to go back to Harvard.

Chapter II

I was bringing George Hill's trunk up from the cellar. It was pretty heavy, and I put it down for a minute outside the library door. I didn't mean to listen, of course, but I couldn't help hearing them inside.

"We've got to be careful," said Jane. "He may be feebleminded, but he isn't blind."

George laughed. "He went to Harvard, didn't he?" he said.

I came in and put the trunk down. My wife was sitting on George's lap. She looked tired, and I felt guilty. It was probably an imposition to ask her to entertain George, because after all he was my guest.

"Who went to Harvard?" I asked idiotically.

"Oh, my God," said Jane.

"Rutherford B. Hayes," said George. "He was the typical Harvard man—dense but energetic."

George often talked that way, probably because he had gone to school at St. Paul's in Garden City instead of the right one. Afterward, of course, he'd run sixty yards against Yale with a broken neck, and he'd made Hedgehog and the Scapula Club, but he never seemed to feel the same way about Harvard as the rest of us.

"Listen, clumsy," said Jane. "How about getting on with that trunk?"

"Well," I said, "I thought I might just sit down here with you two for a minute and have a drink. My feet hurt."

"Never mind about your feet," said Jane. "You get that trunk out in the car. George and I have to start right away if we're going to get to New York before it's dark."

"You're going to New York?" I asked. "You and George?"

"Just for the week-end," said George. "You don't mind, do you?"

"Of course not," I said, "but some people might think it was a little odd. You know how it is in Boston."

"My God," said Jane, "I think he's jealous!"

"Of old George?" That made me laugh. I knew a lot of things had changed since I was at Harvard, but of course there were a lot of other things that never changed. I hadn't quite liked George's remark about Rutherford B. Hayes, who, incidentally had only gone to the law school, but he was my best friend and I knew he was a gentleman. He might be wrong about some things, but he'd be right about the important ones, and that was what really mattered.

They came out while I was still strapping the trunk onto the car, and climbed into the front seat. George started the motor.

"Good-bye," I said. "Have a good time."

"Good-bye, darling," said Jane. "Don't forget to put the cat out."

It was like Jane to think about the cat, even when she was tired and upset. I smiled as I watched the car dropping out of sight down the drive. Things often work out a lot better than you have any business to hope they will.

WOLCOTT GIBBS

"FOR WHOM THE GONG SOUNDS"

(With apologies, somewhat, to Mr. Hemingway)

Robert Jordan snapped the lock of his revolver, made certain the machine-gun at his hip was handy, gripped his màquina and continued to crawl up the Guadarrama hills on his belly. Robert Jordan grinned. You're almost there, he told himself. He'd been telling himself things like that all day. Robert Jordan was hunching over a rocky ledge now, hanging on by the bristles of his chest. The warm Spanish earth scraped his belly. Robert Jordan could feel a pine-cone in his navel. It was a resinous pine-cone, the kind they grow in Catalan. These people, Robert Jordan thought, turn out to be people. There's no getting away from that. Sure there isn't. Hell, no.

A gypsy was sitting on a rock strumming a guitar. With one bare foot he practiced range-finding with a sub-machine gun. The other foot lay idly on his màquina. The gypsy's face was the color of old Virginia ham.

"Salud," Robert Jordan said.

Fernando eyed him through the barrel of a Lewis gun. Robert Jordan made certain his Mauser was uncocked. The gypsy's voice was like golden Amontillado gurgling out of a wineskin.

"Thou wast of the street car, camarada?"

"Come no? Why not?" Robert Jordan thought of the last street car he had blown up. They had found arms and legs all over the roofs. One femur had gone as far as Valladolid.

"Quien sabe," said Jacinto. "Who knows."

"Each according to each," said Ignacio. "Street cars I have a boredom of. We have heard what we have heard. Sí. Yes." He flung some hand grenades into a nose-bag, trampling them firmly with his rope-soled feet.

"Hombre," said Anselmo, squinting down the barrel of a 45mm. gun. "One goes to the cave."

"Bueno," said Robert Jordan. "Good."

Robert Jordan and the gypsy continued to scrabble up the hill past a deserted saw-mill. Juanito burrowed his way, Andalusian fashion, into a pile of saw-dust, and emerged after a little while, grinning sweatily. Robert Jordan opened his pack, making sure that all was as it had been. He unlocked the grommet, untied the drawstrings, uncoiled the insulating wire and tossed the caber. His groping fingers came in reassuring contact with a bunch of bayonets. His automatic pistols were safe, so were the hand grenades, the old French '75 and his father's sawed-off shot-gun. His father had been a preacher, a man of God back in Ohio. He drew forth a bottle of TNT and a quart of Haig and Haig. It might come in handy when the time came for blowing up the boardwalk. He studied the bottle of Haig and Haig and thought, no. They'll take me for a fascist. A bloody fascist, that's what they'll take me for. He put the bottle of Haig and Haig back into the bandolier of ammunition, screwing it down with a grenade pin, a belaying pin and a Skull and Bones pin. Then he got out a magnum of Courvoisier. This is more their stuff, he said to himself. Then to make sure, he pulled out a carton of Abdullas and a box of Corona Coronas. That was all he had in his knapsack except, of course, his sleeping bag, a case of Old Grandad, three pairs of rope-soled shoes and an asbestos suit for when he blew up the boardwalk.

An old man sat at the mouth of the cave guarding the entrance with a Mauser, a Howitzer, a Winchester and a Fly-swatter.

"Salud, camarada," said the old man.

"Equally," said Robert Jordan, then added, "Hola!" for good measure.

"Thou. Thou was of the street-car?"

"Wast."

He is old, Robert Jordan said to himself. And the gypsy is old, too, and some day I will be old. But I'm not old yet, not yet, I'm not old.

"He knows of which whereof he speaks of, old one," the gypsy was saying.

"Qué va, young one."

"It makes well to joke, old one."

"Pass, middle-aged one."

263

The mouth of the cave was camouflaged by a curtain of saddle-blankets, matadores' capes and the soles of old espadrilles. Inside it smelt of man-sweat, acrid and brown . . . horse-sweat sweet and magenta. There was the leathery smell of leather and the coppery smell of copper and borne in on the clear night air came the distant smell of skunk.

The wife of Pablo was stirring frijoles in a Catalonian wineskin. She wore rope-soled shoes and a belt of hand grenades. Over her magnificent buttocks swung a 16th Century cannon taken from the Escorial.

"I obscenity in the obscenity of thy unprintable obscenity," said Pilar.

"This is the Ingles of the street car. He of the boardwalk to come soon."

"I obscenity in the unprintable of the milk of all street cars." The woman was stirring the steaming mess with the horns of a Mura bull. She stared at Robert Jordan then smiled. "Obscenity, obscenity, obscenity," she said, not unkindly.

"Qué va," said Robert Jordan. "Bueno. Good."

"Menos mal," said El Sordo. "Not so good."

"Go unprint thyself," said Pilar. The gypsy went outside and unprinted himself.

The girl with the shaved head filled a tin pail full of petite marmite and handed it to him and she gave him a great swig from the wine-skin and he chewed the succulent bits of horsemeat and they said nothing.

And now Esteban stood beside him on the rim of the gorge. This is it, Robert Jordan said to himself. I believe this is it. I did not think it was this to be it but it seems to be it, alright. Robert Jordan spat down the gorge. Pablo watched the fast disappearing globule of man-saliva then slowly, softly spat down the gorge. Pilar said obscenity thy saliva then she too spat down the gorge. This time it was Pablo's gorge.

The girl was walking beside him.

"Hola, Ingles," she said. "Hello, English."

"Equally, guapa," said Robert Jordan.

"Qué va," said the girl.

"Rabbit."

Robert Jordan pulled the pistol lanyard up, cocked his maquina and tightened the ropes of his rope-soled shoes.

"Vamos," he said. "Let's go."

"Sí," said Maria. "Yes."

They walked on in silence until they came to a rocky ledge. There were rough rocks and thistles and a wild growth of Spanish dagger. Robert Jordan spread his buffalo robe out for himself and allowed Maria to lie near him on a bed of nettles. The earth moved.

"Rabbit," said Robert Jordan. "Hast aught?"

"Nay, naught."

"Maria," he said. "Mary. Little shaved head."

"Let me go with thee and be thy rabbit."

The earth moved again. This time it was a regular earthquake. Californians would have called it a temblor.

Robert Jordan had reached the boardwalk. He lay in the gorse and rubble. He had his infernal machine beside him, some hand grenades, a blunderbuss, an arquebus and a greyhound bus. His maquina was held securely in his teeth. Across the ravine Anselmo was sniping off sentries as they passed.

Listen, Robert Jordan said to himself, only the fascist bombs made so much noise he couldn't hear. You had to do what you did. If you don't do what you do now you'll never do what you do now. Now now you won't. Sure it does. He lashed the wire through the rings of the cotter pins of the release levers of the wires of the main spring of the coil, insulating it with a piece cut off the bottom of his rope-soled shoes.

What about the others . . . Eladio and Ignacio . . . Anselmo and St. Elmo? And Rabbit? I wonder how Rabbit is. Stop that now. This is no time to think about Rabbit . . . Or rabbits. Better think about something else. Think about llamas. It's better to breathe, he thought. It's always much better to breathe. Sure it is. The time was gradually, inevitably drawing near. Someone in the valley was singing an old Catalonian song. A plane crashed quietly overhead. Robert Jordan lay still and listened for the gong to sound.

CORNELIA OTIS SKINNER

There they were, two dark wandering atoms.

Uncle Habbakuk, though one of the legendary, far-wandering Gants, and full to the bung of their dark, illimitable madness, was of but average height, being only eight or nine feet high. He lifted his form from one of his characteristic disgusting, unsavory, and nauseating messes which he had been Wolfeing in the most extraordinary manner. It consisted of old iron filings, chopped twine, oats, and clippings *hachis* from the *Times* classified ads section. With his hard, bony forefinger he prodded Aunt Liz. Ceaselessly he prodded her, hungrily, savagely, with maniacal intensity. But she gave no sign. She was lost (Oh lost! lost, who shall point out the path?) in a dream of time.

"Phuh! Phuh!" howled Uncle Habbakuk, the goat-cry welling up like a madness out of the vine of his throat. "Phuh! Phuh! Ow-ooh! *Beep.*"

In the telling phrase of Baedeker, the situation "offered little that need detain the tourist," but Uncle Habbakuk, with demonic, fore-fingered energy, continued to lift up his idiotic, wordless and exultant howl. It was monstrous, yet somehow lovely, not to say fated, this gaunt confrontation of these two lonely atoms. . . . How strange and full of mystery life is? One passes another in the street, or a face flashes past as the great huge train-projectiles of America hurtle by, in all their thrill and menace, over the old brown earth, and the soul fills with sadness and irrecoverable memories. Why is this? Is it because we are the sons of our fathers and the nieces and nephews of our aunts and uncles?

Who will answer our questions, satisfy our furious impatience, allay our elemental desires, soothe our tormented unrest, and check our heavy baggage? Who?

"Beep!" barked Uncle Habbakuk in his coruscation and indefinite way. "What is man that thou—*whah!*—art mindful of him?"

"Whoo-oop," chirped and sniggled Aunt Liz. Sly and enigmatic, she picked up a morsel of bread and hurled it savagely upon the table, with a gesture old as time itself, and secret with the secretiveness of a thousand secretive, lovely and mysterious women, all secret. Then she relapsed into her dream of time. She was entranced in one of her brooding and incalculable states** (O the States, the States of America, O Alabama, Arizona, Arkansas and California; O Colorado, Connecticut, Delaware and Florida; O Georgia, Idaho, Illinois, and Indiana; O Iowa, Kansas, Kentucky and Louisiana; O Maine, Maryland, Massachusetts and Michigan; O Minnesota, Mississippi, Missouri and Montana; O Nebraska, Nevada, New Hampshire and New Jersey; O New Mexico, New York, North Carolina and North Dakota; O Ohio, Oklahoma, Oregon and Pennsylvania; O Rhode Island, South Carolina, South Dakota and Tennessee; O Texas, Utah, Vermont and Virginia; O Washington, West Virginia, Wisconsin and Wyoming; and O! O! O! O! the District of Columbia!)

At this very moment, so pregnant and prescient with the huge warp of fate and chance, the dark, terrific weaving of the threads of time and destiny, there was heard one of the loveliest and most haunting of all sounds, a sound to echo in the ears of Americans forever, surging in the adyts of their souls and drumming in the conduits of their blood. The doorbell tinkled.

"A moment's—*beep!*—peace for all of us before we die," snarled, bellowed and croaked gaunt Uncle Habbakuk, prodding himself violently in the midriff with his hard bony forefinger. "Give the goat-cry!"

"Phuh-phuh. Owooh! *Beep!*" came the goat-cry from without, and Aunt Liz opened the door. It was he, the youth, of the tribe of the Gants, eleven feet, eight inches high, with slabsided cheeks, high, white, integrated forehead, long, savage, naked-looking ears, thirty-two teeth, one nose, and that strange, familiar, native alien expression to all the Gants, wandering forever and the earth again. It was the youth but no less was it Jason and Faustus and Antaeus and Dronos and Telemachus and Synopsis and all those shining young heroes who want merely to know everything, who have hungered amid the *gewirr* of life and sought their fathers in the congeries of the compacted habitations of man, hot for the alexing of our cure and amorous of the unknown river and a thousand furious streets.

With a loose and powerful gesture Uncle Habbakuk, in frenzied despair, luminous hope and frantic entreaty, welcomed the youth, snuffling.

"Where have you *been,* youth? Have you touched, tasted, heard *and* seen *everything?* Have you *smelt* everything? Have you come from out the wilderness, the buried past, the lost *America?* Are you bringing up Father out of the *River?* Have you done any delicate diving for *Greeks?* Tell me, have you embraced *life* and *devoured* it? Tell me! Open the adyts of your soul. Beep."

"Beep," chirped the youth somberly. "I have been making mad journeys, peril-fraught and passion-laden, on the Hudson River Day Line, eight journeys, watching my lost, million-visaged brothers and sisters. I have been lying (in my upper berth) above good-looking women in the lower berth on a thousand train-wanderings. They were all of them tall and sensual-looking Jewesses, all proud, potent, amber, dark, and enigmatic. I always felt they would not rebuff me if I spoke to them, but yet I did not speak. Later on, however, I wondered about their lives. Yet I have been with a thousand women, their amber thighs spread amorously in bright golden hay. After ten thousand others have I lusted, making a total score of eleven thousand. O hot amorous flesh of sinful women!

"Pent in my dark soul I have sought in many countries my heart's hope and my father's land, the lost but unforgotten half of my own soul. In the fierce, splendid, strange and secret North have I sought; and, on the other hand, in the secret, strange, splendid and fierce South. In the fatal web of the City strangely and bitterly have I savoured the strange and bitter miracles of life; and at N.Y.U. (Downtown Branch) have I wondered darkly at the dark wonder of man's destiny. Amid this phantasmagoric chaos, in a thousand little sleeping towns built across the land (O my America! O my!) I have pursued my soul's desire, looking for a stone, a leaf, a door we never found, feeling my Faustian life intolerably in my entrails. I have quivered a thousand times in sensual terror and ecstatic joy as the 5:07 pulled in. I have felt a wild and mournful sorrow at the thought, the wonderful thought that everything I have seen and known (and have I not known and seen all that is to be seen and known upon this dark, brooding continent?) has come out of my

268

own life, is indeed I, or me, the youth eternal, many-visaged and many-volumed.

"Whatever it may be, I have sought it through my kaleidoscopic days and velvet-and duvetyn-breasted nights, and, in my dark, illimitable madness, in my insatiate and huge unrest, in my appalling and obscene fancies in my haunting and lonely memories (for we are all lonely), in my grotesque, abominable and frenzied prodigalities, I have always cried aloud—"

"Whoo-oops," gargled, snorted and snuffled Aunt Liz from out her dream of time.

"What is it that we know so well and cannot speak?" continued the youth, striding a thousand strides across a hundred floors. "What is it that we speak so well and cannot know?" Why this ceaseless pullulation stirring in my branching veins, not to be stilled even by the white small bite and tigerish clasp of secret women, of whom I have had one thousand in round figures? Whence the savagery, the hunger and the fear? I have sought the answer in four hundred and twelve libraries, including the Mercantile, the 42nd Street Public, the Muhlenberg Branch, and Brooklyn—ah, Brooklyn, vast, mysterious, and never-to-be forgotten Brooklyn and its congeries of swarming, unfathomable life, O Brooklyn! I have read in ten years at least 20,000 books, devouring them twelve hours a day, no holidays, 400 pages to a book, or in other words—X and I am furiously fond of other words—I have read 33 pages a minute, or a page every two seconds. Yet during this very same period I managed with ease to prowl ten thousand wintry, barren and accursed streets, to lie, you recollect, with one thousand women, and take any number of train-trips (Oh! the dark earth stroking forever past the huge projectile!) This it is to be a Gant! Questing my destiny lying ever before me, I have been life's beauty-drunken lover, and kept women and notebooks in a hundred cities, yet have I never found the door or turned the knob or slipped the bolt or torn off the leaf or crossed the road or climbed the fence. I have seen fury riding in the mountains, but who will show me the door?"

At this point Aunt Liz, with broad, placid, harmonious strokes, swam up out of her dream of time, and, uttering no words, arose from her chair. Out of her dark pocket, pursuing characteristically her underlip, she drew a Key and with it opened, at the back of the room, a Door. The youth followed her within. Before him stretched, extended and was a combined and compacted pantry, provision-chamber, larder, storage-cellar and ice-house.

From the ceiling hung flitches of bacon, strings of onions, and festoons of confetti. On the walls hung and depended the carcasses and bodies of rabbits, hares, sheep, lambs, chamois and gazelles. On smaller hooks and on shelves were stored partridges, grouse, plovers, geese, turkeys, pheasants, snipe, capercalzie, royal bustards, and three penguins designed by Walt Disney. On the floor at the rear lay sadly a small whale. Ranged on shelves were seasonings and condiments—serried boxes, packages, canisters, bottles and jars of salt (including Epsom, Kruschen, Enos, Seidlitz and Glauber), cinnamon, saffron, olive oil, palm oil, colza oil, ground-nut oil, castor oil, and just the old oil. In a tumultuous variety of breadboxes were to be seen cornbread, rye, gluten, white, whole wheat, buns, pumpernickel, scones, bannocks, oatcakes, biscuits, *croissants* and *brioches,* and many cubic feet of permanently buttered toast. In the section reserved for *charcuterie* the youth's brilliant eye fell on quantities of ham, tongue, smoked eels, salami, pork, caviar, smoked salmon, bacon, pimentoes, gherkins, pickles, *foie gras,* anchovies, sardines, *liverwurst, cervelat, chipolata, mortadello,* and striking quantities of plain boloney. In an enormous icebox rested crates, boxes and cases of eggs deriving from the hen, the sparrow, the bantam, the duck, the turkey, the goose, and the bald-headed eagle. In another, nested in ice, lay, deliciously, salmon, trout, carp, perch, eels, pike, herrings, mackerel, and shark's-fins. The cheeses included Roquefort, Camembert, Cheddar, Cheshire, Stilton, Gorgonzola, Brie, Saint-Marcellin, and Snacks. Of fruit and vegetables there were too many for recounting in this volume, but the curious reader will find them in the sequel, "Eugene on the River in a Catboat."

Dazzled, astounded, bewildered and amazed, the youth, thoroughly surprised, surveyed these riches, then turned, in a paroxysm of joy, to Aunt Liz, forever brooding on her dream of time.

"*This,* then, was the Key," he ululated, "*this* the Door from which the Wolfe cannot be kept!" Triumphantly he snatched a few dozen forks, knives, spoons, and can-openers and set to, his long, weary and unfathomable quest at last over forever.

"Beep," chuckled Uncle Habbakuk gauntly.

CLIFTON FADIMAN

"REQUIEM FOR A NOUN, OR INTRUDER IN THE DUSK"

(What Can Come of Trying to Read William Faulkner
While Minding a Child, or Vice Versa)

The cold Brussels sprout rolled off the page of the book I was reading and lay inert and defunctive in my lap. Turning my head with a leisure at least three-fourths impotent rage, I saw him standing there holding the toy with which he had catapulted the vegetable, or rather the reverse, the toy first then the fat insolent fist clutching it and then above that the bland defiant face beneath the shock of black hair like tangible gas. It, the toy, was one of those cardboard funnels with a trigger near the point for firing a small celluloid ball. Letting the cold Brussels sprout lie there in my lap for him to absorb or anyhow apprehend rebuke from, I took a pull at a Scotch highball I had had in my hand and then set it down on the end table beside me.

"So instead of losing the shooter which would have been a mercy you had to lose the ball," I said, fixing with a stern eye what I had fathered out of all sentient and biding dust; remembering with that retroactive memory by which we count chimes seconds and even minutes after they have struck (recapitulate, even, the very grinding of the bowels of the clock before and during and after) the cunning furtive click, clicks rather, which perception should have told me then already were not the trigger plied but the icebox opened. "Even a boy of five going on six should have more respect for his father if not for food," I said, now picking the cold Brussels sprout out of my lap and setting it—not dropping it, setting it—in an ashtray; thinking how across the wax bland treachery of the kitchen linoleum were now in all likelihood distributed the remnants of string beans and cold potatoes and maybe even tapioca. "You're no son of mine."

I took up the thread of the book again or tried to: the weft of legitimate kinship that was intricate enough without the obbligato of that dark other: the sixteenths and thirty-seconds and even sixty-fourths of dishonoring cousinships brewed out of the violable blood by the ineffaceable errant lusts. Then I heard another click; a faint metallic rejoinder that this time was neither the trigger nor the icebox but the front door opened and then shut. Through the window I saw him picking his way over the season's soiled and sun-frayed vestiges of snow like shreds of rotted lace, the cheap upended toy cone in one hand and a child's cardboard suitcase in the other, toward the road.

I dropped the book and went out after him who had forgotten not only that I was in shirtsleeves but that my braces hung down over my flanks in twin festoons. "Where are you going?" I called, my voice expostulant and forlorn on the warm numb air. Then I caught it: caught it in the succinct outrage of the suitcase and the prim churning rear and marching heels as well: I had said he was no son of mine, and so he was leaving a house not only where he was not wanted but where he did not even belong.

"I see," I said in that shocked clarity with which we perceive the truth instantaneous and entire out of the very astonishment that refuses to acknowledge it. "Just as you now cannot be sure of any roof you belong more than half under, you figure there is no house-top from which you might not as well begin to shout it. Is that it?"

Something was trying to tell me something. Watching him turn off on the road—and that not only with the ostensible declaration of vagabondage but already its very assumption, attaining as though with a single footfall the very apotheosis of wandering just as with a single shutting of a door he had that of renunciation and farewell —watching him turn off on it, the road, in the direction of the Permisangs', our nearest neighbors, I thought *Wait; no; what I said was not enough for him to leave the house on; it must have been the blurted inscrutable chance confirmation of something he already knew, and was half able to assess, either out of the blown facts of boyhood or pure male divination or both.*

"What is it you know?" I said springing forward over the delicate squalor of the snow and falling in beside the boy. "Does any man come to the house to see your mother when I'm away, that you know of?" Thinking *We are mocked, first by the old mammalian*

*snare, then, snared, by the final unilaterality of all flesh to which
birth is given; not only not knowing when we may be cuckolded, but
not even sure that in the veins of the very bantling we dandle does
not flow the miscreant sniggering wayward blood.*

"I get it now," I said, catching in the undeviating face just as I
had in the prim back and marching heels the steady articulation
of disdain. "Cuckoldry is something of which the victim may be as
guilty as the wrong-doers. That's what you're thinking? That by
letting in this taint upon our heritage I am as accountable as she
or they who have been its actual avatars. More. Though the foe
may survive, the sleeping sentinel must be shot. Is that it?"

"You talk funny."

Mother-and-daughter blood conspires in the old mammalian office. Father-and-son blood vies in the ancient phallic enmity. I
caught him by the arm and we scuffled in the snow. "I will be
heard," I said, holding him now as though we might be dancing,
my voice intimate and furious against the furious sibilance of our
feet in the snow. Thinking how revelation had had to be inherent
in the very vegetable scraps to which venery was probably that
instant contriving to abandon me, the cold boiled despair of whatever already featureless suburban Wednesday Thursday or Saturday supper the shot green was the remainder. "I see another thing,"
I panted, cursing my helplessness to curse whoever it was had given
him blood and wind. Thinking *He's glad; glad to credit what is
always secretly fostered and fermented out of the vats of childhood
fantasy anyway (for all childhood must conceive a substitute for
the father that has conceived it (finding that other inconceivable?);
thinking He is walking in a nursery fairy tale to find the king his
sire.* "Just as I said to you 'You're no son of mine' so now you
answer back 'Neither are you any father to me.' "

The scherzo of violence ended as abruptly as it had begun. He
broke away and walked on, after retrieving the toy he had dropped
and adjusting his grip on the suitcase which he had not, this time
faster and more urgently.

The last light was seeping out of the shabby sky, after the hemor-
rhage of sunset. High in the west where the fierce constellations soon
would wheel, the evening star in single bombast burned and burned.

The boy passed the Permisangs' without going in, then passed the Kellers'. Maybe he's heading for the McCullums', I thought, but he passed their house too. Then he, we, neared the Jelliffs'. He's got to be going there, his search will end there, I thought. Because that was the last house this side of the tracks. And because *something was trying to tell me something.*

"Were you maybe thinking of what you heard said about Mrs. Jelliff and me having relations in Spuyten Duyvil?" I said in rapid frantic speculation. "But they were talking about mutual kin—nothing else." The boy said nothing. But I had sensed it instant and complete: the boy felt that, whatever of offense his mother may or may not have given, his father had given provocation; and out of the old embattled malehood, it was the hairy ineluctable Him whose guilt and shame he was going to hold preponderant. *Because now I remembered.*

"So it's Mrs. Jelliff—Sue Jelliff—and me you have got this all mixed up with," I said, figuring he must, in that fat sly nocturnal stealth that took him creeping up and down the stairs to listen when he should have been in bed, certainly have heard his mother exclaiming to his father behind that bedroom door it had been vain to close since it was not sound-proof: "I saw you. I saw that with Sue. There may not be anything between you but you'd like there to be! Maybe there is at that!"

Now like a dentist forced to ruin sound enamel to reach decayed I had to risk telling him what he did not know to keep what he assuredly did in relative control.

"This is what happened on the night in question," I said. "It was under the mistletoe, during the Holidays, at the Jelliffs'. Wait! I will be heard out! See your father as he is, but see him in no baser light. He has his arms around his neighbor's wife. It is evening, in the heat and huddled spiced felicity of the year's end, under the mistletoe (where as well as anywhere else the thirsting and exasperated flesh might be visited by the futile pangs and jets of later lust, the omnivorous aches of fifty and forty and even thirty-five to seize what may be the last of the allotted lips). Your father seems to prolong beyond its usual moment's span that custom's usufruct. Only for an instant, but in that instant letting trickle through the fissures of appearance what your mother and probably Rudy Jelliff too saw as an earnest of a flood that would have devoured that house and one four doors away."

A moon hung over the eastern roofs like a phantasmal bladder. Somewhere an icicle crashed and splintered, fruits of the day's thaw.

"So now I've got it straight," I said. "Just as through some nameless father your mother has cuckolded me (you think), so through one of Rudy Jelliff's five sons I have probably cuckolded him. Which would give you at least a half brother under that roof where under ours you have none at all. So you balance out one miscreance with another, and find your rightful kin in our poor weft of all the teeming random bonded sentient dust."

Shifting the grip, the boy walked on past the Jelliffs'. Before him —the tracks; and beyond that—the other side of the tracks. And now out of whatever reserve capacity for astonished incredulity may yet have remained I prepared to face this last and ultimate outrage. But he didn't cross. Along our own side of the tracks ran a road which the boy turned left on. He paused before a lighted house near the corner, a white cottage with a shingle in the window which I knew from familiarity to read, "Viola Pruett, Piano Lessons," and which, like a violently unscrambled pattern on a screen, now came to focus.

Memory adumbrates just as expectation recalls. The name on the shingle made audible to listening recollection the last words of the boy's mother as she'd left, which had fallen short then of the threshold of hearing. ". . . Pruett," I remembered now. "He's going to have supper and stay with Buzzie Pruett overnight. . . . Can take a few things with him in that little suitcase of his. If Mrs. Pruett phones about it, just say I'll take him over when I get back," I recalled now in that chime-counting recapitulation of retroactive memory—better than which I could not have been expected to do. Because the eternal Who-instructs might have got through to the whiskey-drinking husband or might have got through to the reader immersed in that prose vertiginous intoxicant and unique, but not to both.

"So that's it," I said. "You couldn't wait till you were taken much less till it was time but had to sneak off by yourself, and that not cross-lots but up the road I've told you a hundred times to keep off even the shoulder of."

The boy had stopped and now appeared to hesitate before the house. He turned around at last, switched the toy and the suitcase in his hands, and started back in the direction he had come.

"What are you going back for now?" I asked.

"More stuff to take in this suitcase," he said. "I was going to just sleep at the Pruetts' overnight, but now I'm going to ask them to let me stay there for good."

PETER DE VRIES

A BIBLIOGRAPHY OF PARODY

(A selected bibliography of books of parody and about parody with special reference to the American literary scene.)

ANTHOLOGIES

Hamilton, Walter B., ed. *Parodies of the Works of English and American Authors.* 6 Vols. London: Reeves and Turner, 1884-1885.

Leonard, R. M., and Jerrold, Walter, eds. *A Century of Parody and Imitation.* London: Oxford University Press, 1913.

McCord, David, ed. *What Cheer.* New York: Coward-McCann, 1945.

Rhys, Ernest, ed. *A New Book of Sense and Nonsense.* London: J. M. Dent & Sons, 1930.

Russell, L., ed. *Parody Party.* London: Hutchinson, 1936.

Saunders, Henry S., ed. *Parodies on Walt Whitman.* New York: American Library Service, 1923.

Squire, J. C., ed. *Apes and Parrots.* London: H. Jenkins Ltd., 1929.

Symons, Arthur, ed. *A Book of Parodies.* London: Blackie, 1908.

Wells, Carolyn, ed. *A Nonsense Anthology.* New York: Scribner's, 1902.

———. *A Parody Anthology.* New York: Scribner's, 1904.

———. *The Book of Humorous Verse.* New York: George H. Doran Co., 1920.

White, E. B. and Katherine S., eds. *A Subtreasury of American Humor.* New York: Coward-McCann Inc., 1941.

Wilson, Albert Edward, ed. *Playwrights in Aspic.* Denver University Press, 1950.

SINGLE-AUTHOR COLLECTIONS

Ade, George. *Fables in Slang.* Chicago and New York: H. S. Stone & Co., 1900.

Bangs, John Kendrick. "The Rise of Hop o' My Thumb," *New Waggings of Old Tales.* Boston: 1888.

———. *The Dreamers, A Club.* New York: 1899.

Bierce, Ambrose. *The Cynic's Word Book.* New York: Doubleday Page & Co., 1906.

Beerbohm, Max. *A Christmas Garland.* New York: E. P. Dutton & Co., 1912.

Benchley, Robert. *Of All Things.* New York: Harper & Bros., 1921.

————. *Pluck and Luck.* New York: Harper & Bros., 1925.

Bunner, Henry Cuyler. *The Poems of H. C. Bunner.* New York: Scribner's Sons, 1896.

Bynner, Witter. *Spectra.* New York: Mitchell Kennerly Co., 1916.

Cary, Phoebe. *Poems and Parodies.* Boston: Ticknor, Reed, and Fields, 1854.

Carryl, Guy Wetmore. *Mother Goose for Grown-Ups.* New York: Harper & Bros., 1900.

Colby, Frank Moore. *Imaginary Obligations.* New York: Dodd Mead & Co., 1904.

Derby, George H. ("John Phoenix") *Phoenixiana.* New York: D. Appleton & Co., 1869.

Ford, Corey. *In the Worst Possible Taste.* New York: Scribner's Sons, 1932.

————. *Meaning No Offense.* New York: John Day Co., 1927.

————. *The John Riddell Murder Case.* New York: Scribner's Sons, 1930.

Gibbs, Wolcott. *Season in the Sun.* New York: Random House, 1937.

Harte, Bret. *Condensed Novels.* New York: James R. Osgood & Co., 1871.

Hoffenstein, Samuel. *Year In You're Out.* New York: Horace Liveright, 1930.

Lardner, Ring. *What of It?* New York: Scribner's Sons, 1925.

Leacock, Stephen. *Frenzied Fiction.* New York: John Lane & Co., 1917.

————. *Nonsense Novels.* New York: Dodd Mead & Co., 1921.

Lippincott, Sara Jane (Grace Greenwood). *Greenwood Leaves.* Boston: 1850.

Norris, Frank. *Frank Norris of "The Wave,"* Stories and Sketches from the San Francisco weekly, 1893 to 1897. San Francisco, 1931.

Osborn, Laughton. *The Vision of Rubeta.* Boston: Weeks, Jordan, and Co., 1838.

Pain, Barry. *Playthings and Parodies.* New York: Cassell Publishing Co., 1892.

Perelman, S. J. *The Best of S. J. Perelman.* New York: Random House, 1947.

Powell, Charles. *Poets in the Nursery.* New York: John Lane & Co., 1920.

Skinner, Cornelia Otis. *Soap Behind the Ears.* New York: Dodd Mead & Co., 1941.

Squire, J. C. *Tricks of the Trade.* New York: G. P. Putnam & Co., 1917.

Stewart, Donald Ogden. *A Parody Outline of History*. New York: Geo. H. Doran Co., 1921.

Taylor, Bayard. *The Echo Club and Other Literary Diversions*. Boston: J. R. Osgood & Co., 1876.

Thurber, James. *The Beast in Me and Other Animals*. New York: Harcourt Brace & Co., 1948.

Untermeyer, Louis. *Collected Parodies*. New York: Harcourt Brace & Co., 1919.

Ward, Christopher. *Foolish Fiction*. New York: Henry Holt Co., 1925.

Wells, Carolyn. *The Re-Echo Club*. New York: Franklin Bigelow Corp., 1913.

White, E. B. *The Second Tree From the Corner*. New York: Harper and Bros., 1954.

Widdemer, Margaret. *A Tree with a Bird in It*. New York: Harcourt Brace & Co., 1922.

ABOUT PARODY

Birss, J. H. "Parodies of American Poets." *Notes and Queries*. CLXII (Jan. 23, 1932).

Blair, Walter. "Burlesque in Nineteenth-Century American Humor." *American Literature*. II, 236-47 (November 1930).

Chancellor, E. Beresford. *Literary Diversions*. London: Dulau & Co., 1925.

Gibbs, Wolcott. *Season in the Sun*. New York: Random House, 1937.

Gosse, Edmund. *More Books on the Table*. London: William Heinemann Ltd., 1923.

Kitchin, G. *A Survey of Burlesque and Parody in English*. Edinburgh: Oliver and Boyd, 1931.

Nock, Albert Jay. "Bret Harte as a Parodist." *Bookman*. LXIX, 250 (May 1929).

Pound, Ezra. *ABC of Reading*. London: G. Routledge & Sons, 1934.

Shepperson, A. B. *The Novel in Motley*. Cambridge, Mass.: Harvard University Press, 1936.

Wyatt, Edith. *Great Companions*. New York: D. Appleton & Co., 1917.